FOR ORGANS, PIANOS & ELECTRONIC KEYBOARDS

E-Z PLAY® TODAY

275

CLASSICA
The 3 B's Bach, Beethoven & Brahms

HAL•LEONARD®
CORPORATION

7777 W. BLUEMOUND RD. P.O. BOX 13819 MILWAUKEE, WI 53213

E-Z Play ® TODAY Music Notation © 1975 HAL LEONARD PUBLISHING CORPORATION
Copyright © 1992 by HAL LEONARD PUBLISHING CORPORATION
International Copyright Secured All Rights Reserved

Contents

Classical Hits - The 3 B's: Bach, Beethoven & Brahms

JOHANN SEBASTIAN BACH

8 Air On The G String

4 Arioso

11 Bist Du Bei Mir

12 Little Fugue in G minor

14 Minuet in G Major
(From NOTEBOOK FOR ANNA
MAGDALENA BACH)

16 Minuet I in G Major
(From NOTEBOOK FOR ANNA
MAGDALENA BACH)

18 Musette
(From NOTEBOOK FOR ANNA
MAGDALENA BACH)

20 Sheep May Safely Graze
(From CANTATA NO. 208)

23 Two-Part Invention in C Major

26 Two-Part Invention in D minor

24 Two-Part Invention in F Major

LUDWIG VAN BEETHOVEN

27 Ecossaise

28 Für Elise

30 Minuet in G Major

31 Piano Concerto No. 5
("Emperor")
(First Movement)

32 Piano Sonata, Op. 13, No. 8 in C minor
("Pathetique")
(Second Movement Theme)

34 Piano Sonata, Op. 27, No. 2
("Moonlight")
(First Movement Theme)

35 Piano Sonata, Op. 49, No. 1 in G minor
(First Movement Theme)

38 Piano Sonatina No. 1 in G Major
(First Movement Theme)

40 Septet
(Third Movement)

43 Symphony No. 5 in C minor
(First Movement Theme)

46 Symphony No. 9
(Fourth Movement, "Ode To Joy")

JOHANNES BRAHMS

52 Academic Festival Overture

56 Ballade in G minor, Op. 118, No. 3

58 Hungarian Dance No. 5

49 Intermezzo, Op. 118, No. 2

60 Intermezzo, Op. 117, No. 3

62 Lullaby
(Wiegenlied)

71 Rhapsody, Op.119, No. 4

64 Symphony No. 1, Op. 68
(Fourth Movement Chorale)

66 Waltz, Op. 39, No. 15

68 Wie Melodien

72 REGISTRATION GUIDE

Arioso

Registration 1

Johann Sebastian Bach

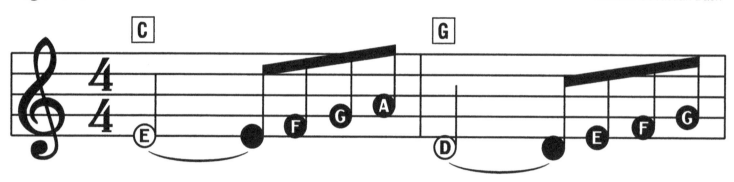

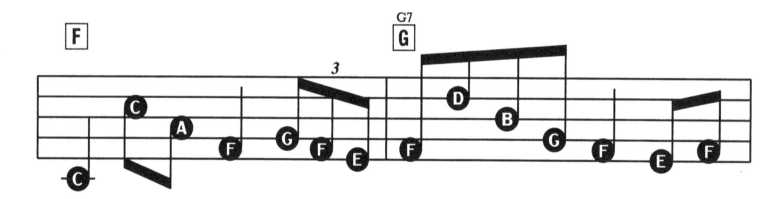

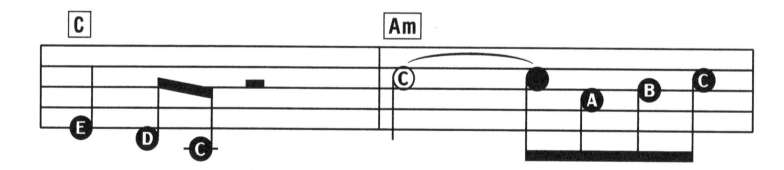

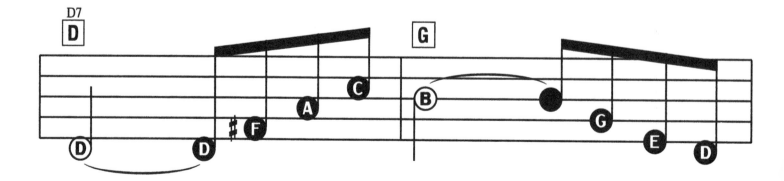

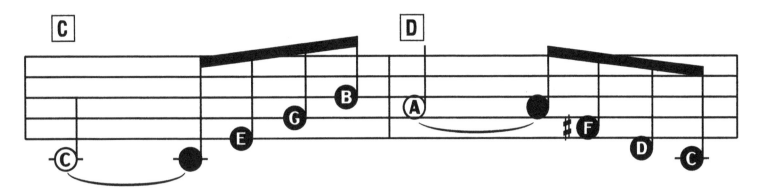

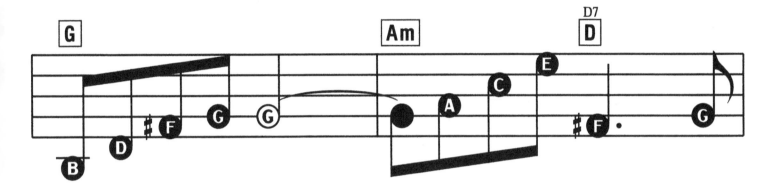

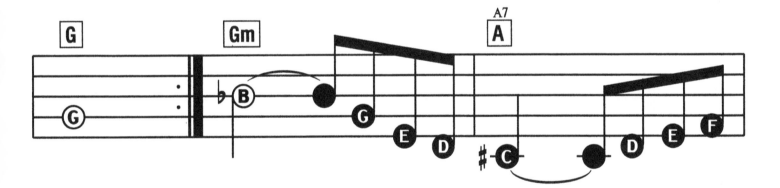

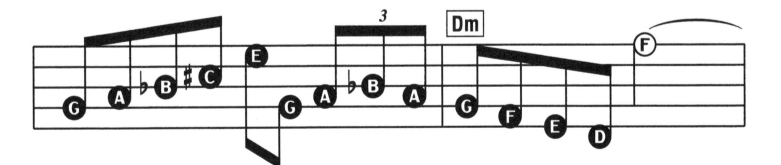

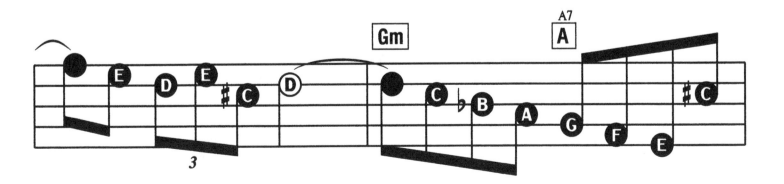

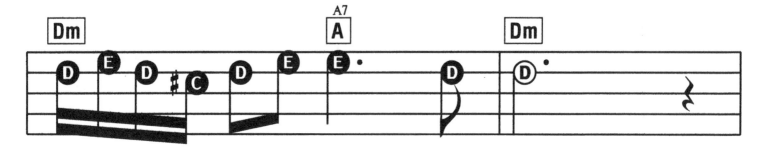

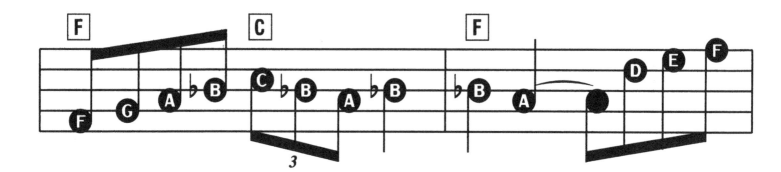

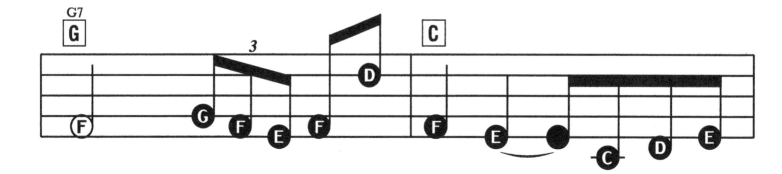

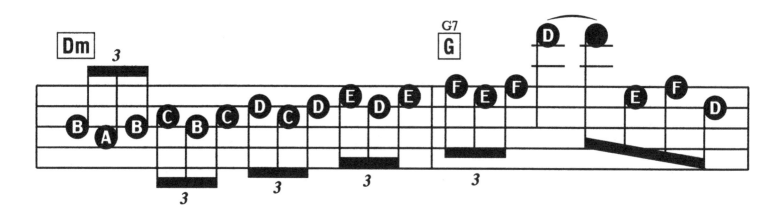

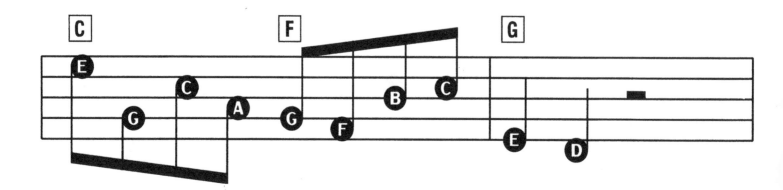

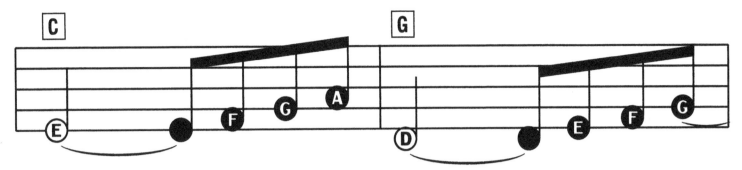

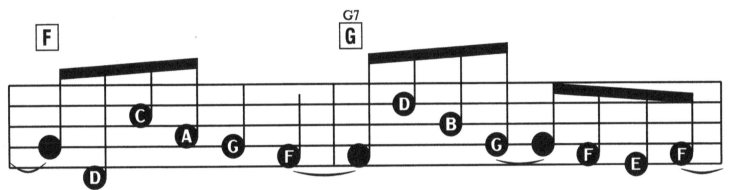

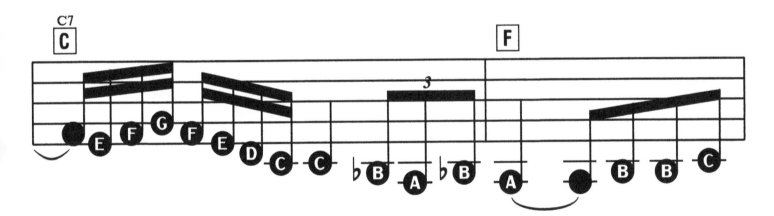

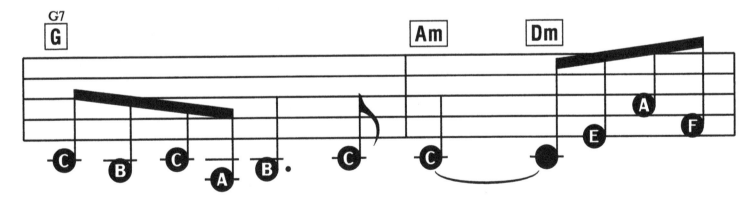

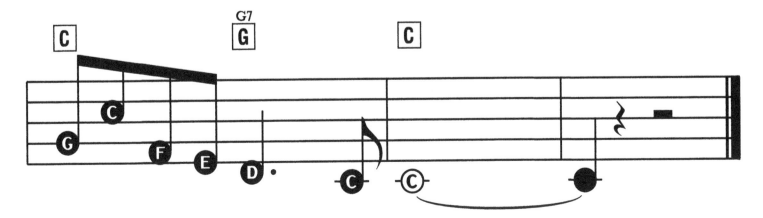

Air On The G String

Registration 10

Johann Sebastian Bach

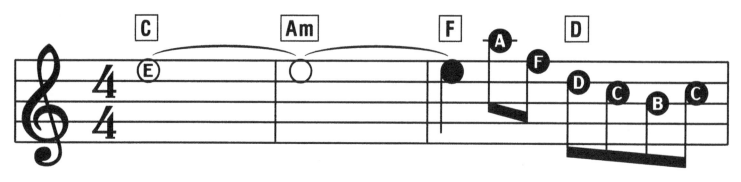

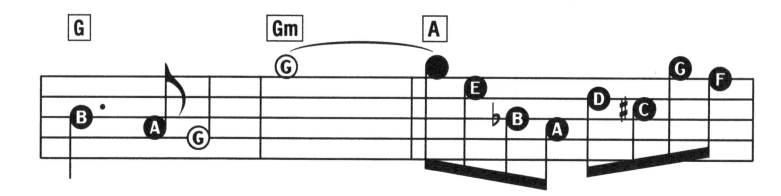

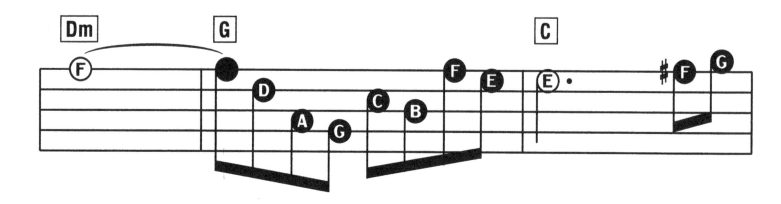

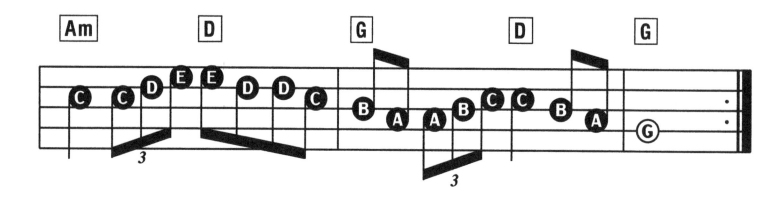

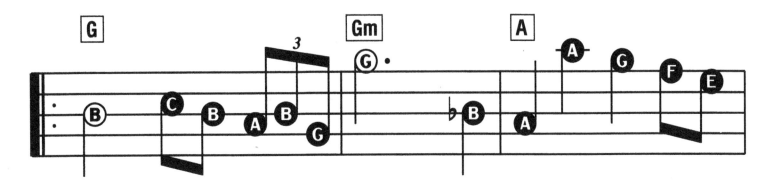

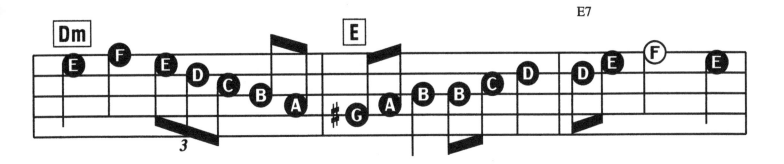

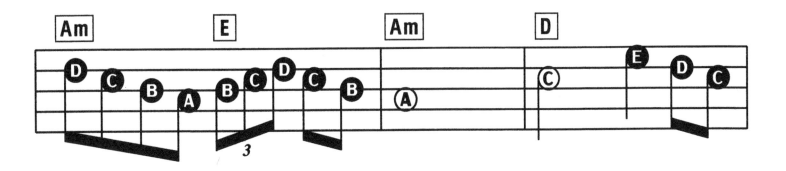

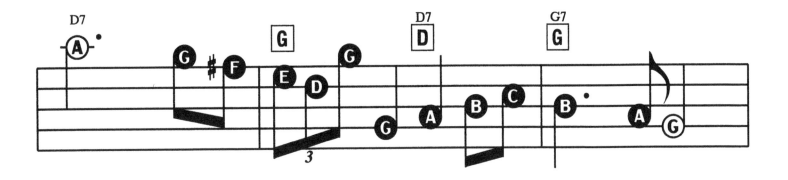

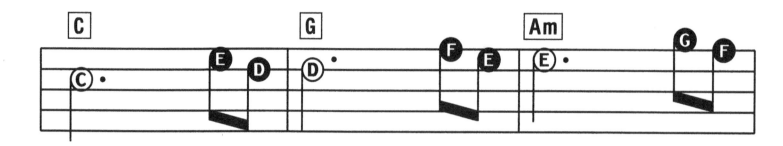

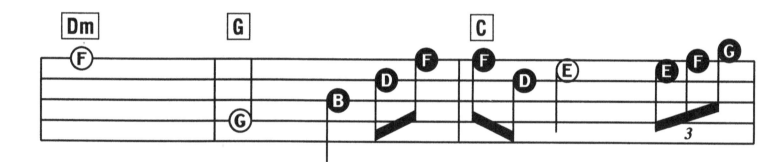

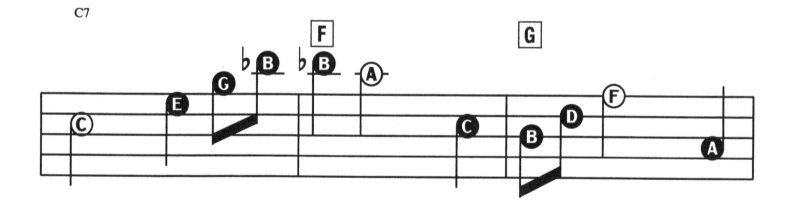

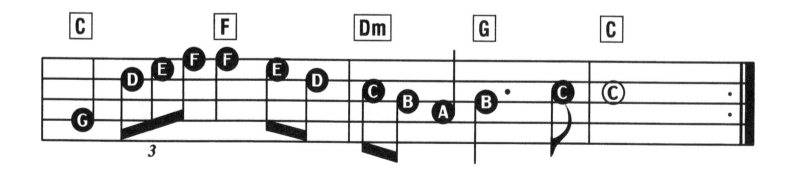

Bist Du Bei Mir

Registration 5

Johann Sebastian Bach

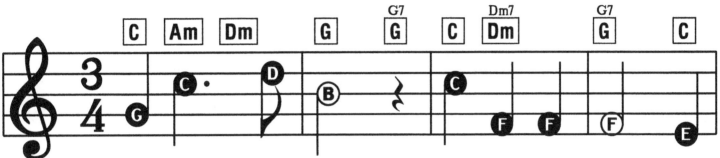

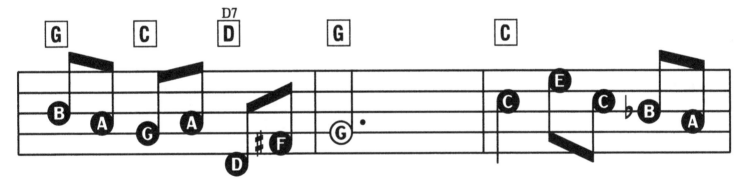

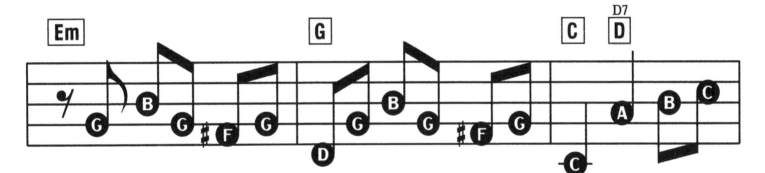

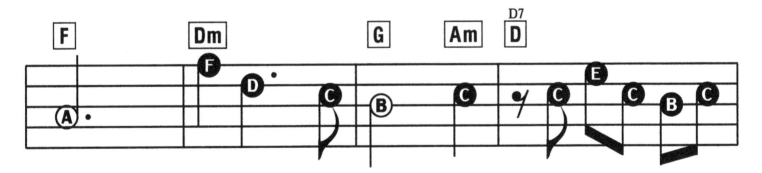

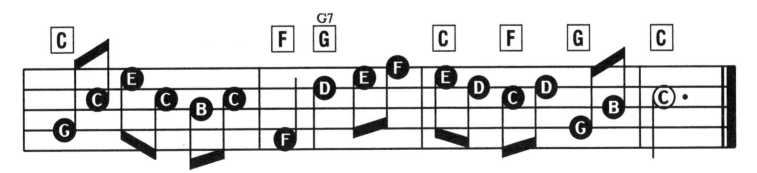

Little Fugue in G minor

Registration 6
Rhythm: Rock

J.S. Bach

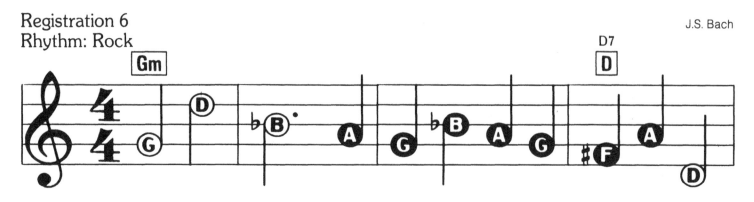

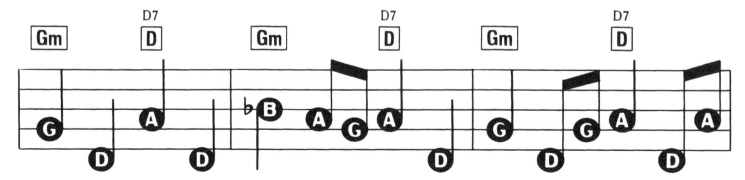

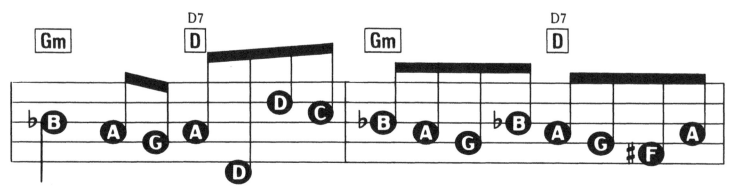

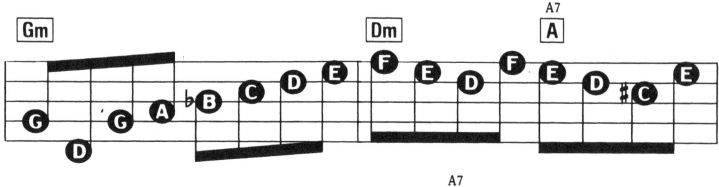

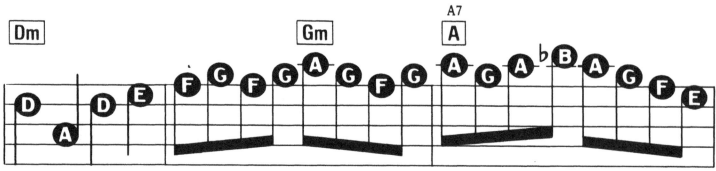

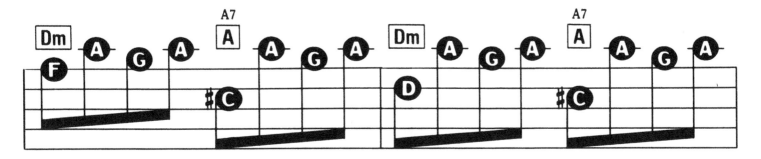

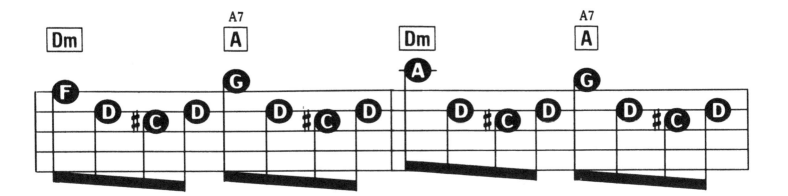

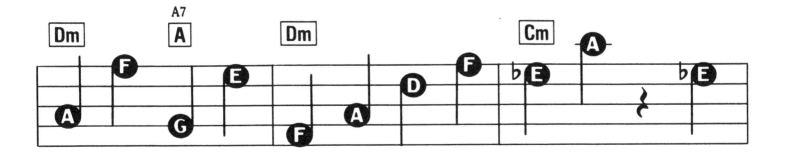

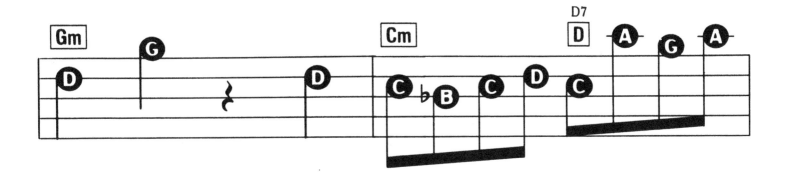

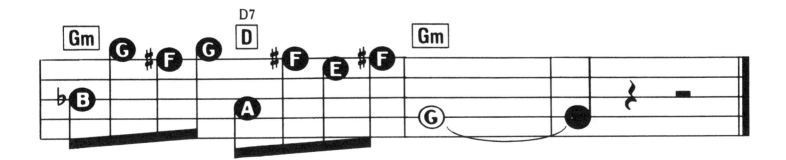

Minuet In G Major
(From NOTEBOOK FOR ANNA MAGDALENA BACH)

Registration 10

J.S. Bach

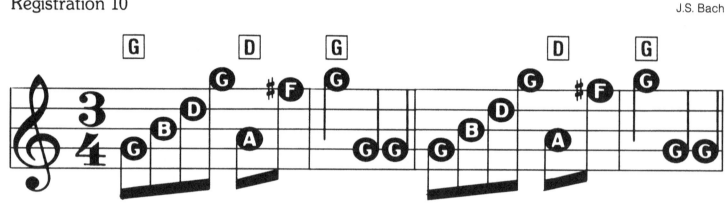

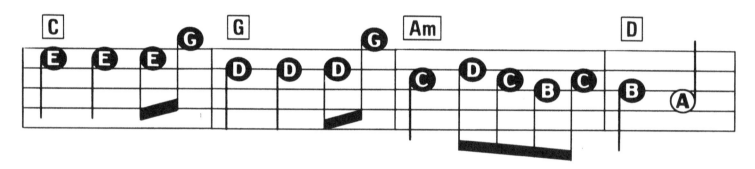

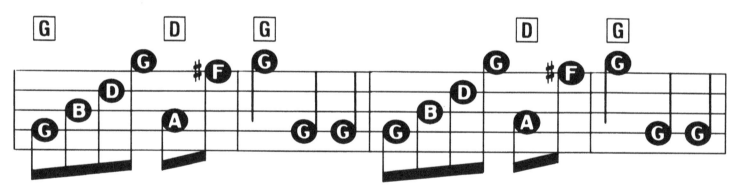

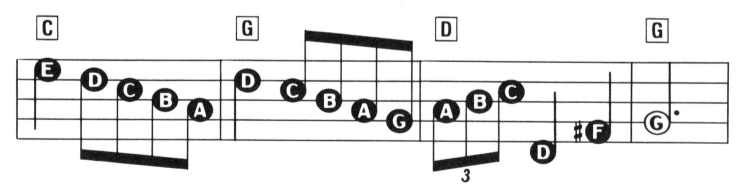

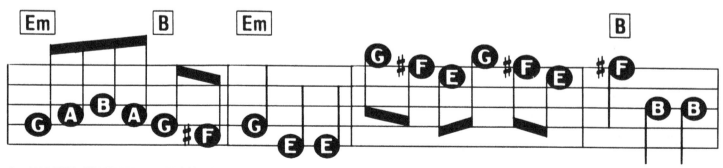

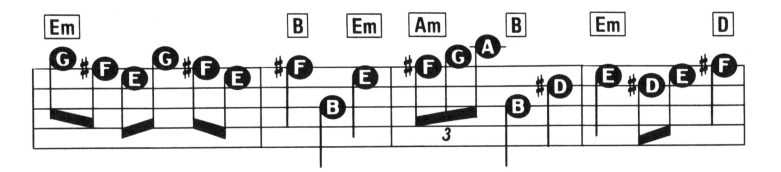

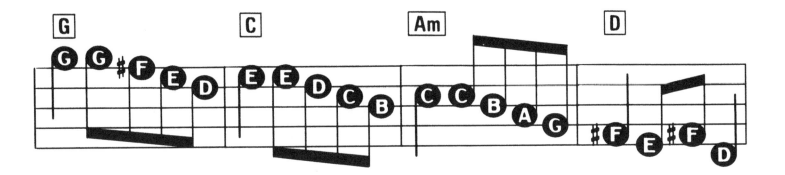

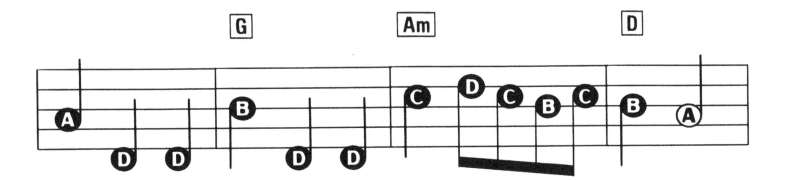

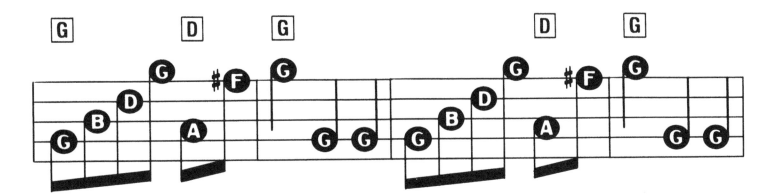

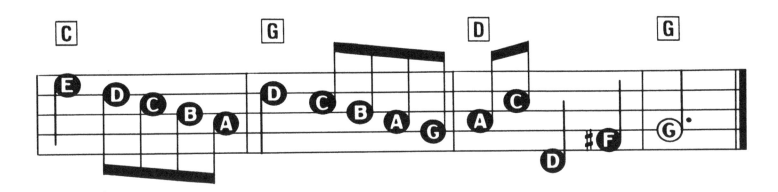

Minuet I in G Major
(From "NOTEBOOK FOR ANNA MAGDALENA BACH")

Registration 8
Rhythm: Waltz

Johann Sebastian Bach

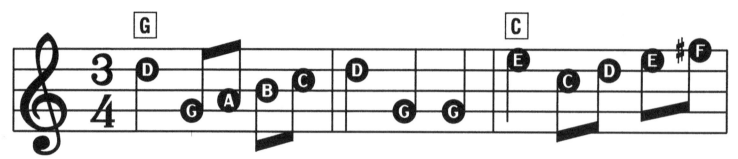

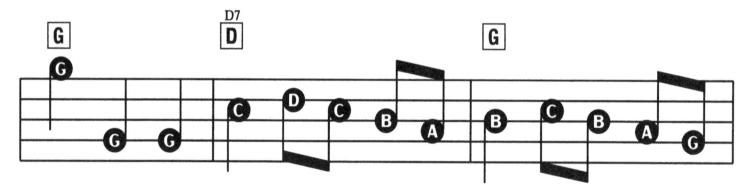

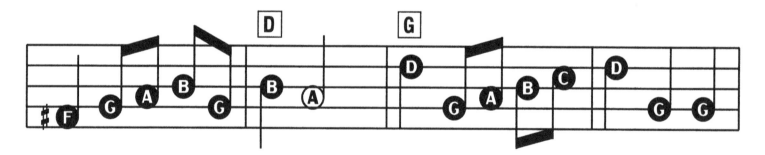

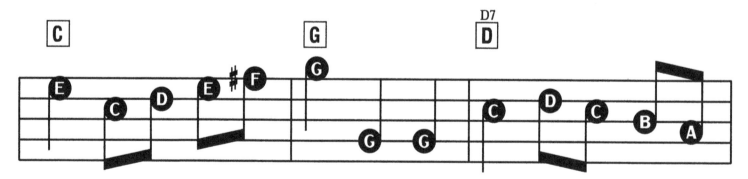

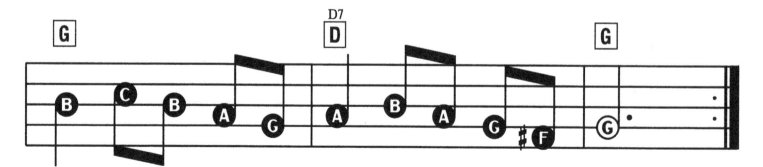

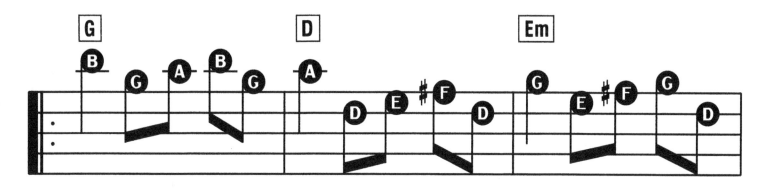

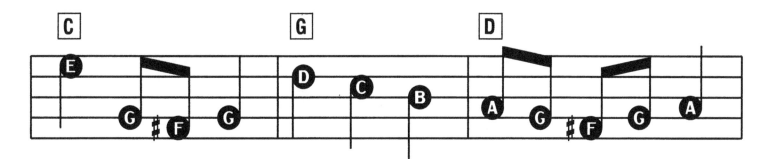

Musette
(From "NOTEBOOK FOR ANNA MAGDALENA BACH")

Registration 2
Rhythm: March or Polka

Johann Sebastian Bach

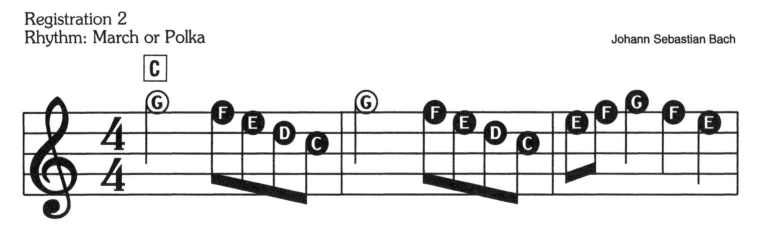

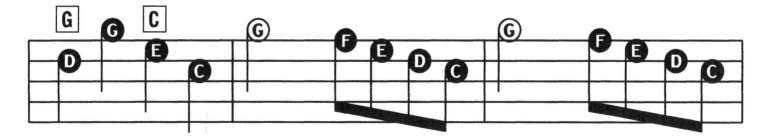

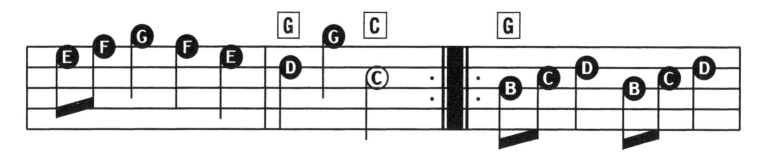

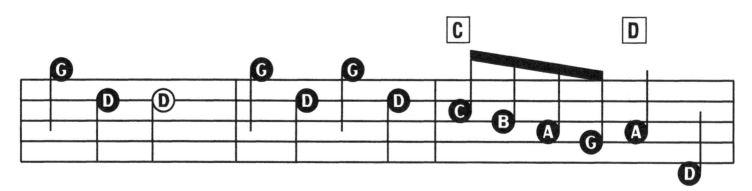

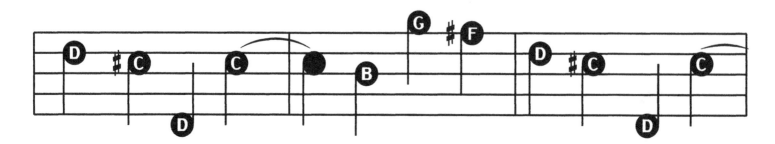

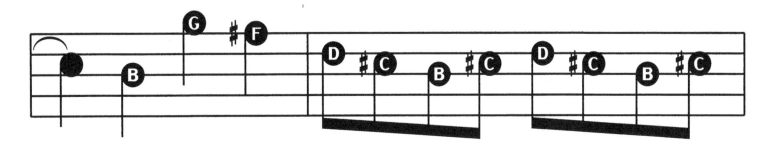

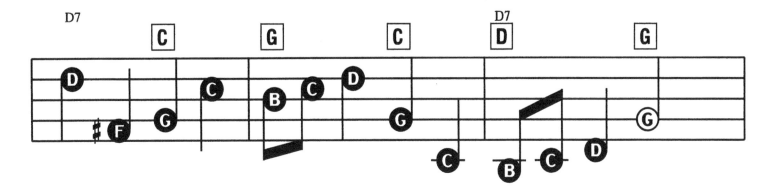

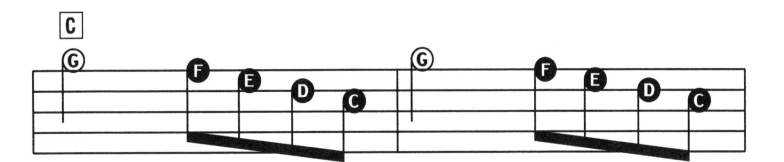

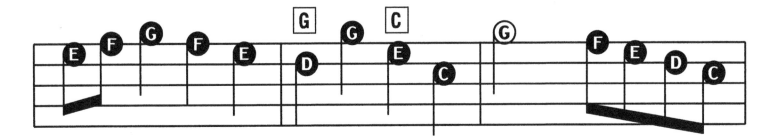

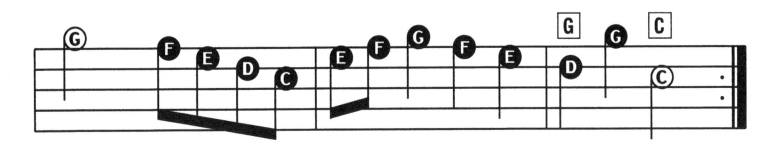

Sheep May Safely Graze

(From CANTATA NO. 208)

Registration 1

Johann Sebastian Bach

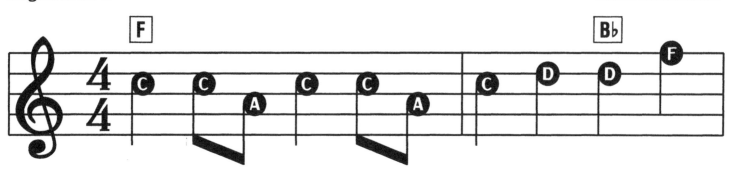

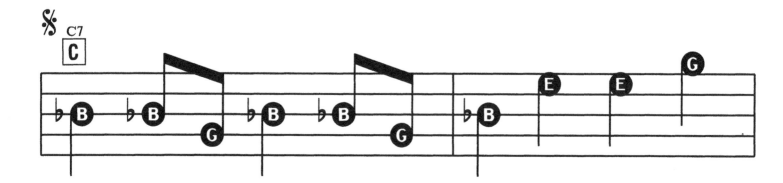

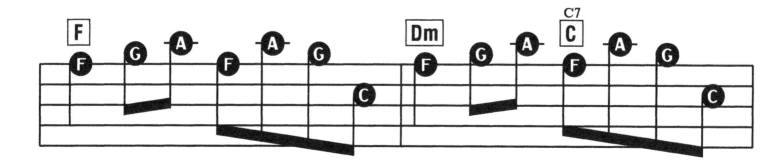

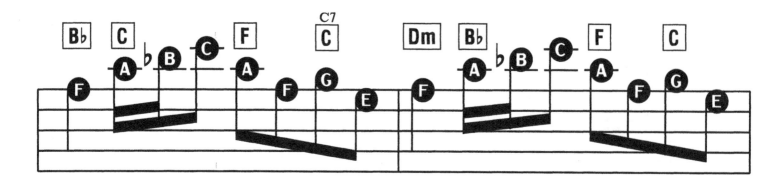

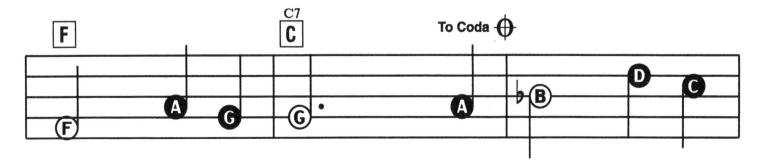

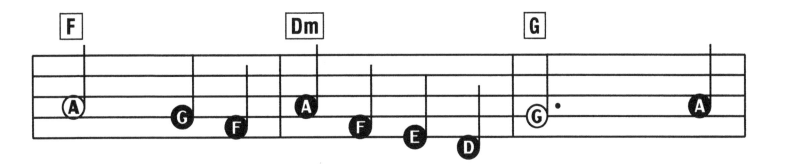

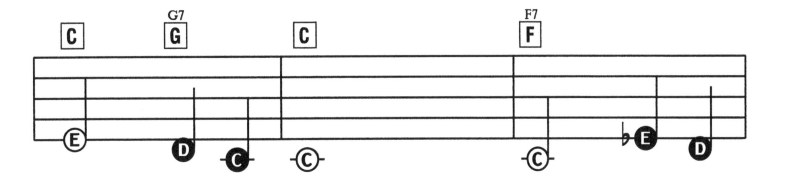

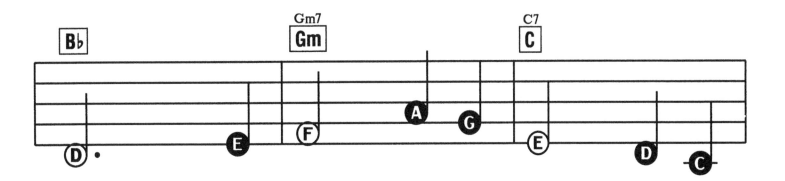

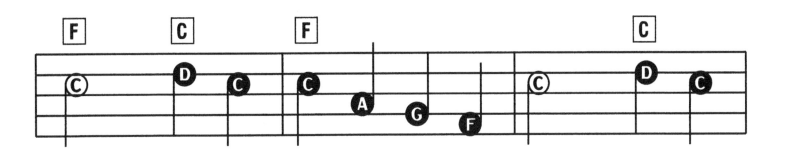

22

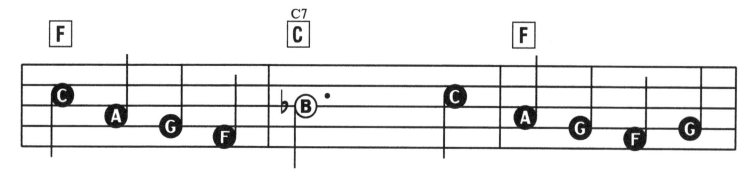

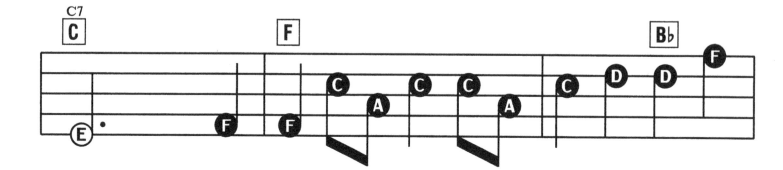

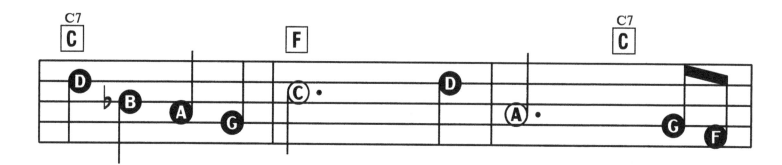

D.S. al Coda
(Return to %
Play to ⊕ and
Skip to Coda)

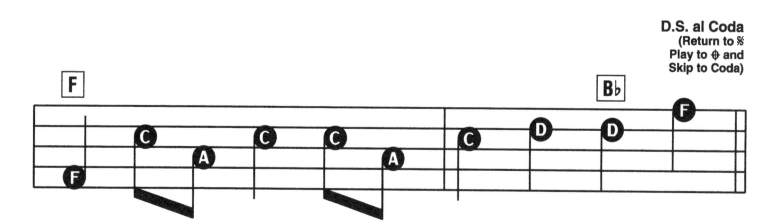

CODA
⊕ F

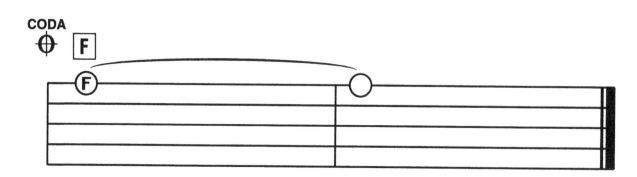

Two-Part Invention In C Major

Registration 6

Johann Sebastian Bach

Two-Part Invention In F Major

Registration 8

Johann Sebastian Bach

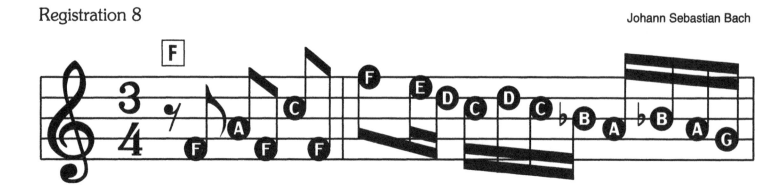

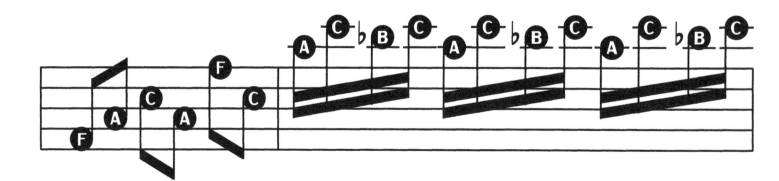

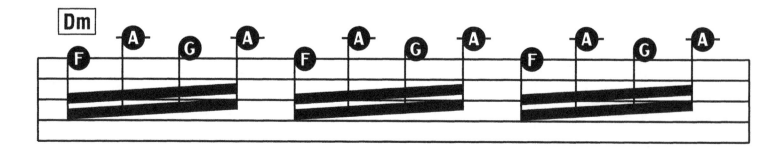

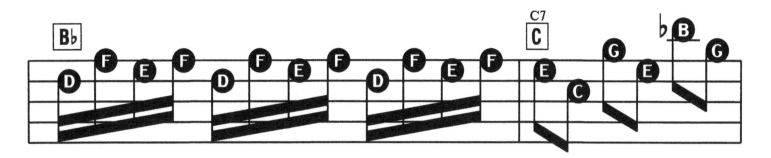

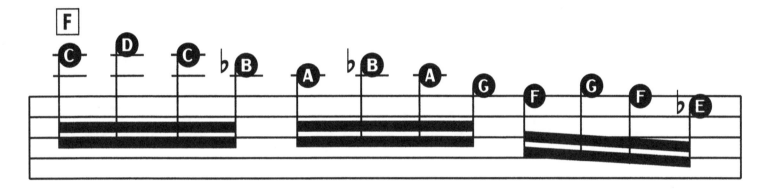

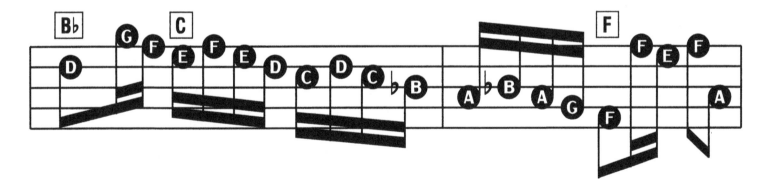

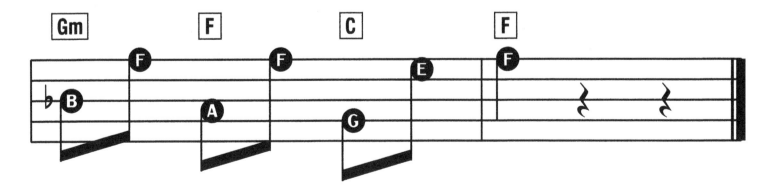

Two-Part Invention In D Minor

Registration 3

Johann Sebastian Bach

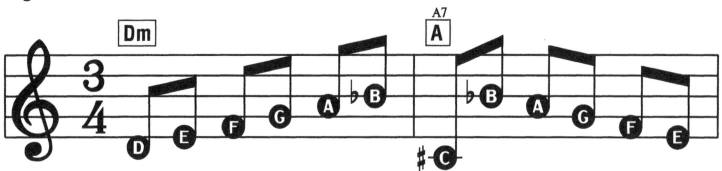

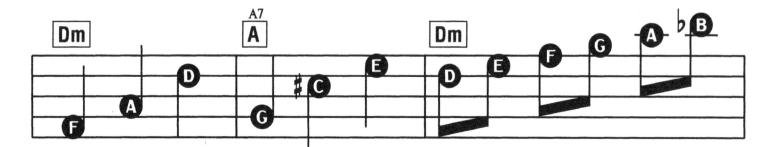

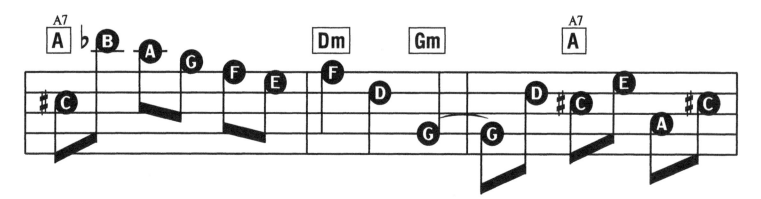

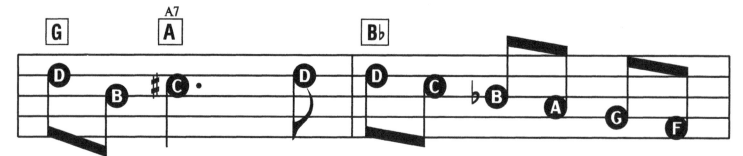

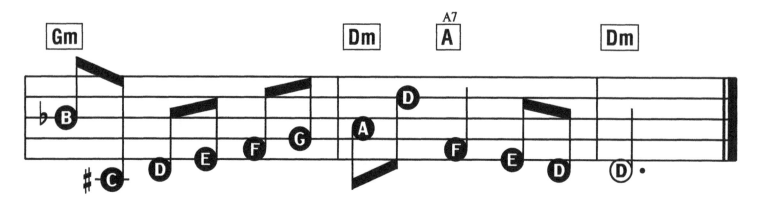

Ecossaise

Registration 8

Ludwig Van Beethoven

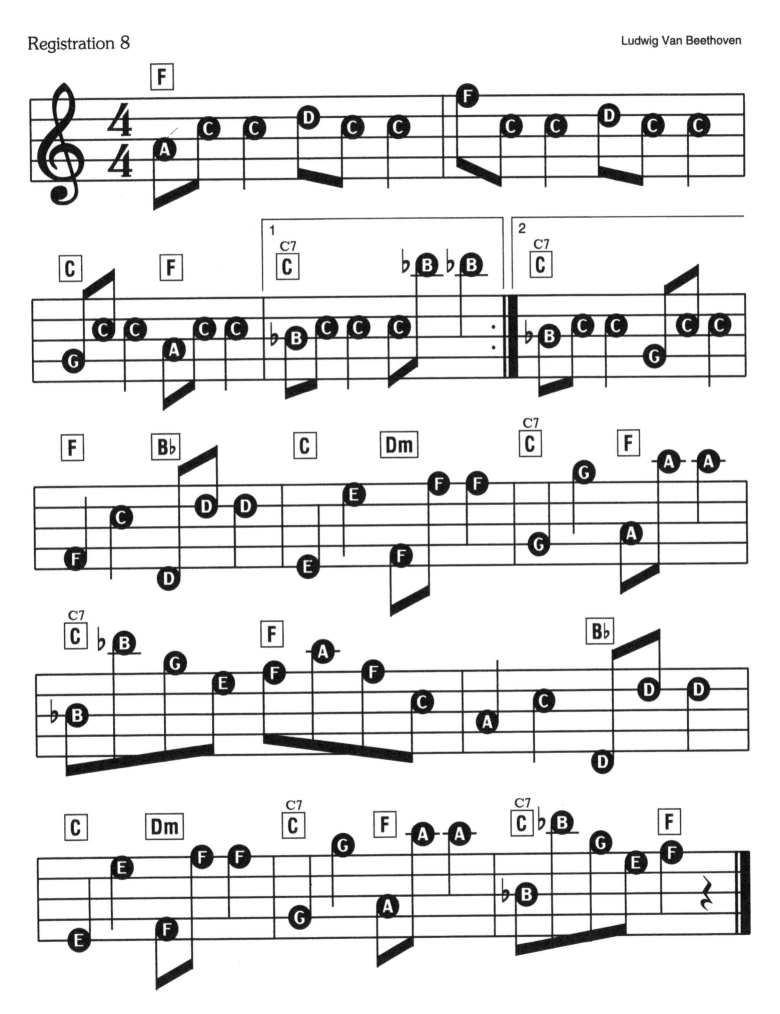

Für Elise

Registration 6

Ludwig Van Beethoven

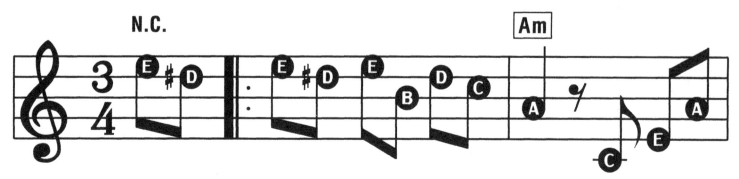

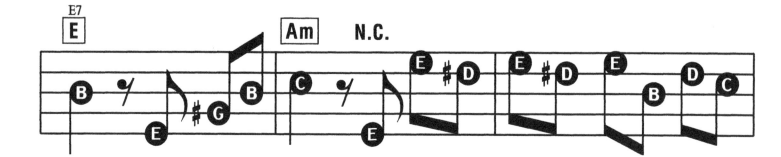

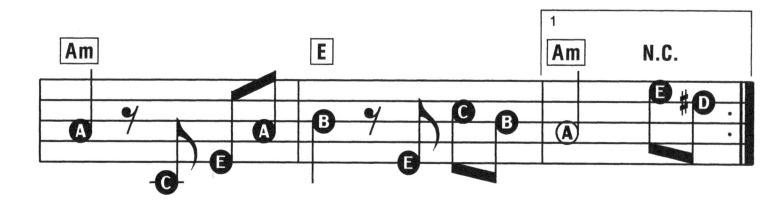

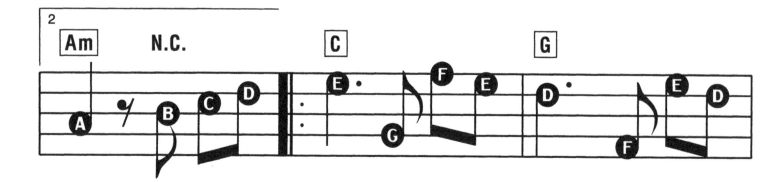

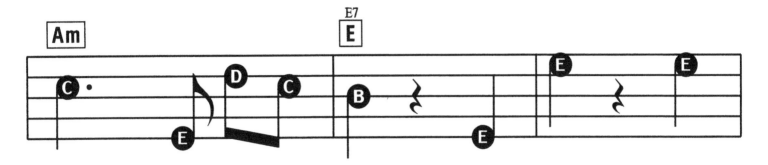

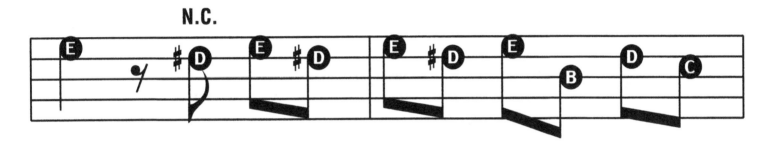

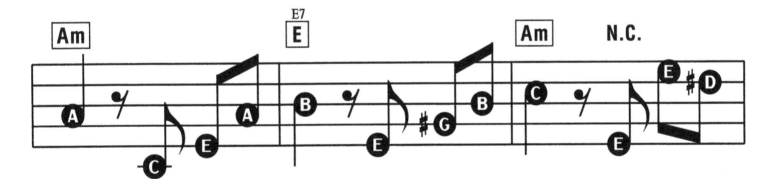

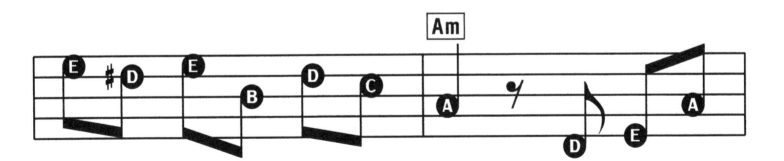

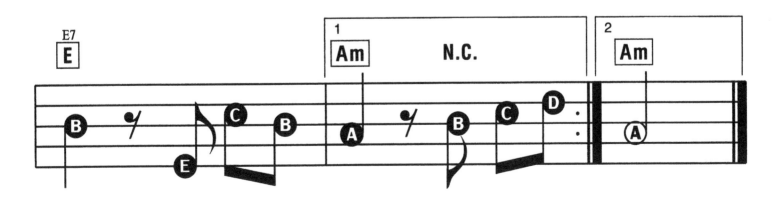

Minuet In G Major

Registration 8
Rhythm: Waltz

Ludwig Van Beethoven

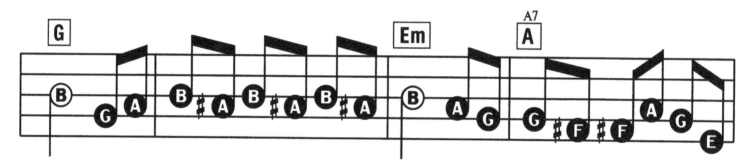

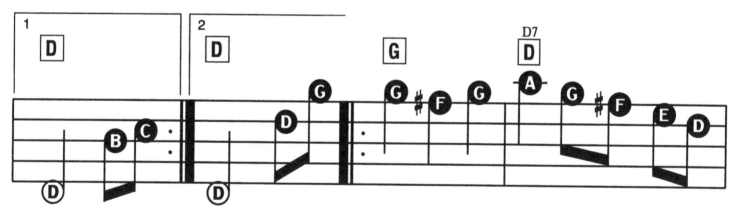

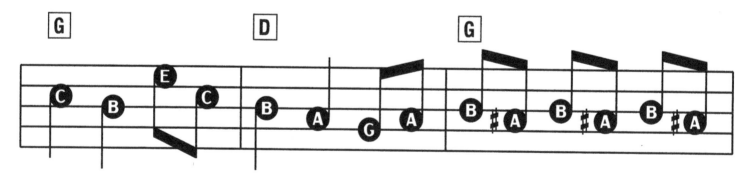

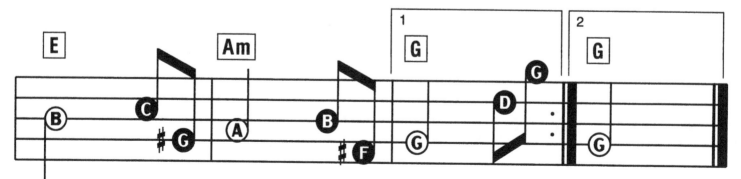

Piano Concerto No. 5
("Emperor")
(First Movement)

Registration 8
Rhythm: March (Optional)

Ludwig van Beethoven

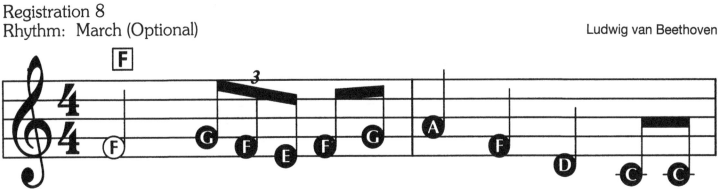

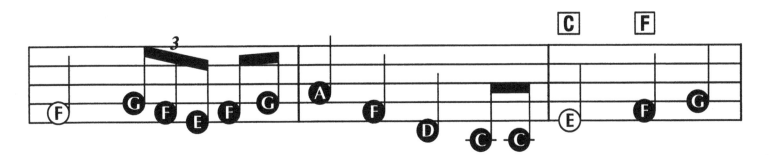

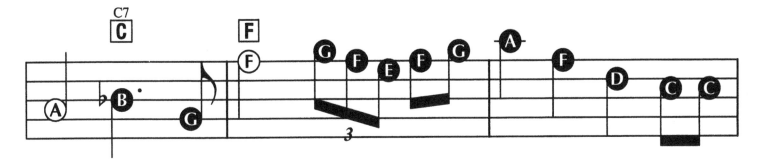

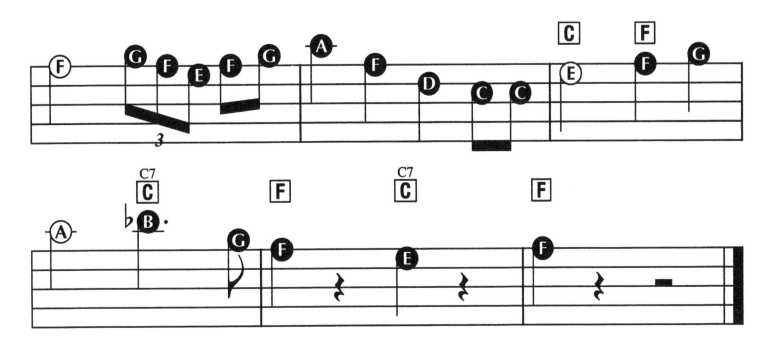

Piano Sonata, Op. 13, No. 8 in C minor
("Pathetique")
(Second Movement Theme)

Ludwig van Beethoven

Registration 6

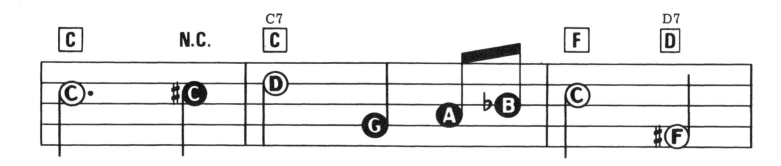

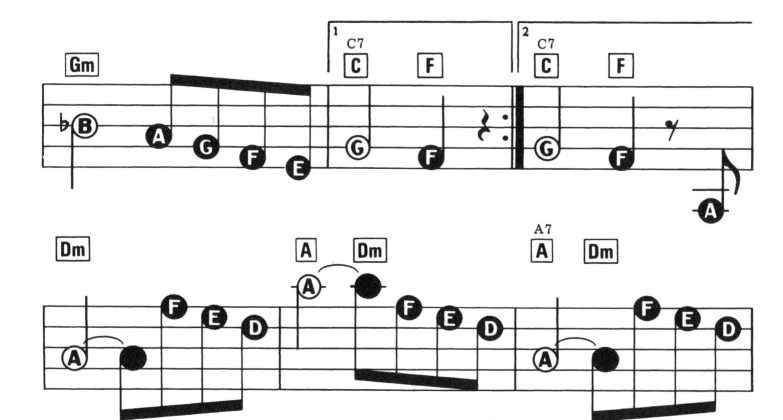

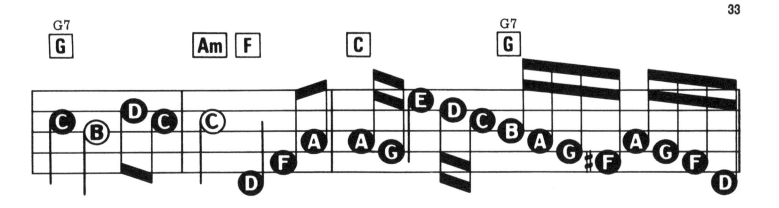

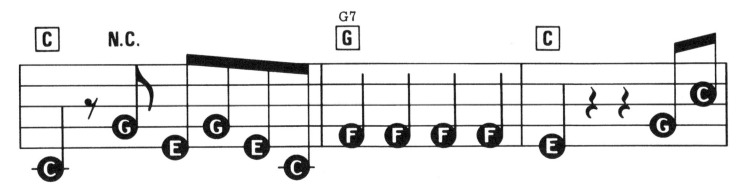

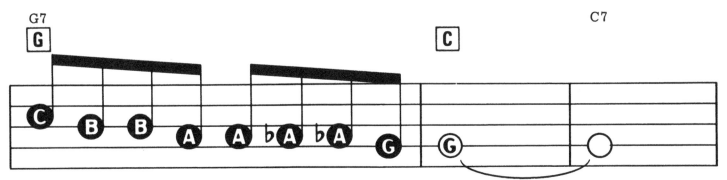

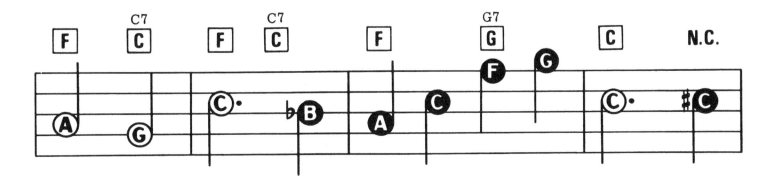

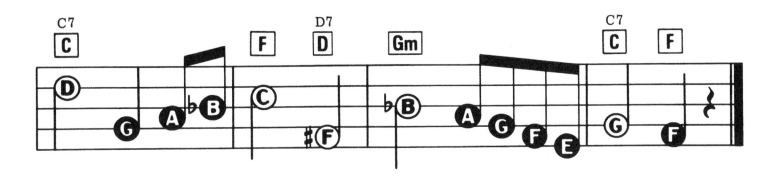

Piano Sonata, Op. 27, No. 2
("Moonlight")
(First Movement Theme)

Registration 8

Ludwig Van Beethoven

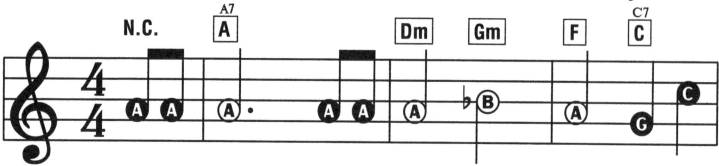

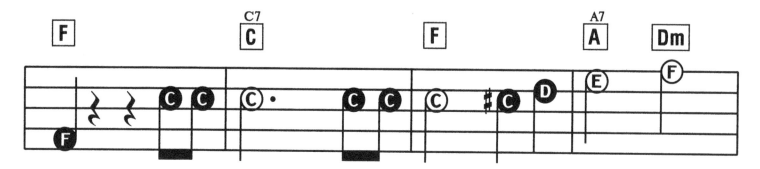

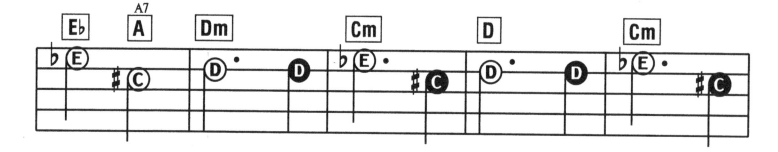

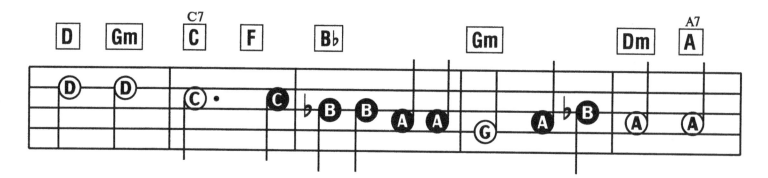

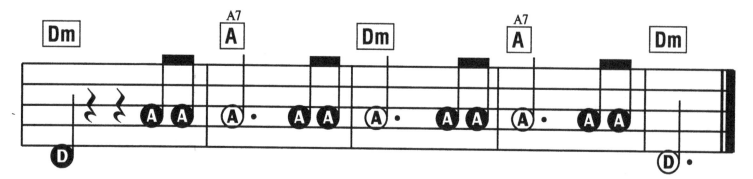

Piano Sonata, Op. 49, No. 1 in G Minor
(First Movement Theme)

Registration 8

Ludwig Van Beethoven

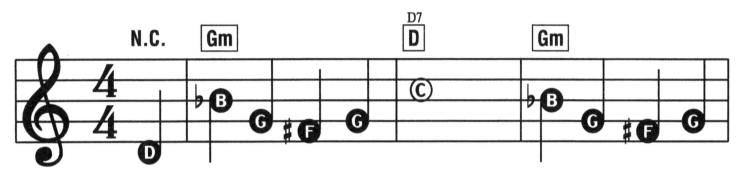

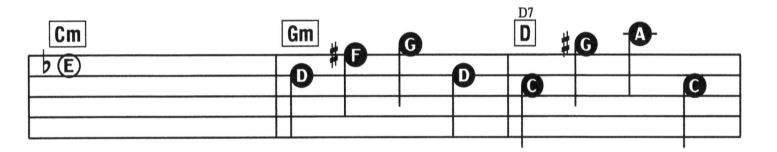

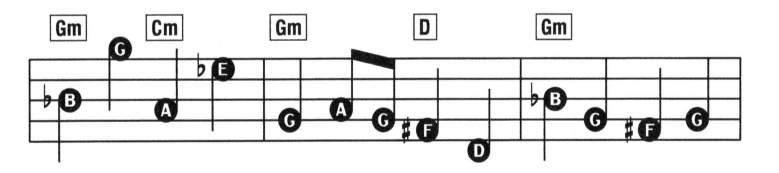

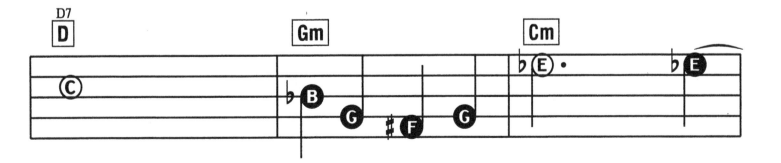

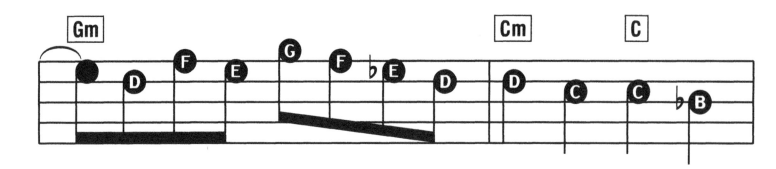

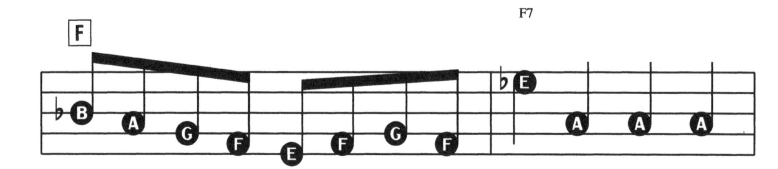

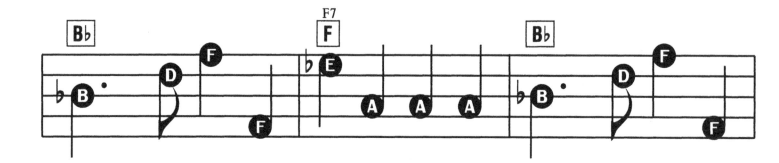

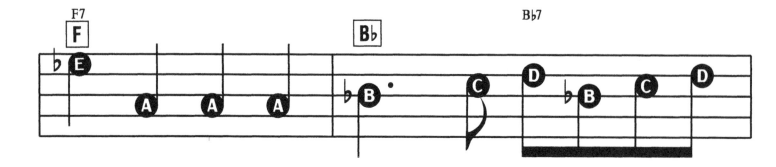

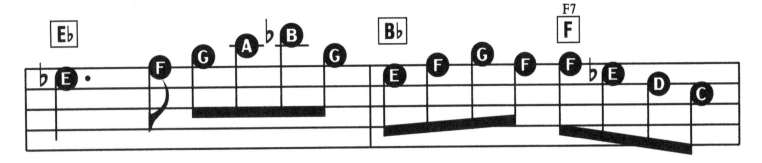

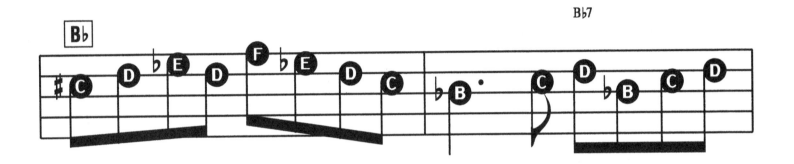

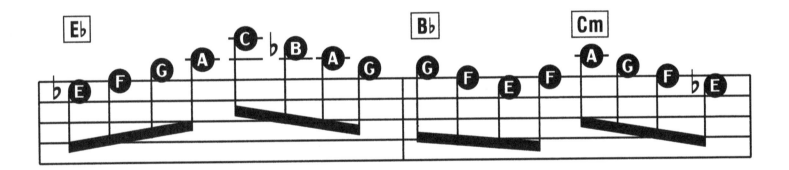

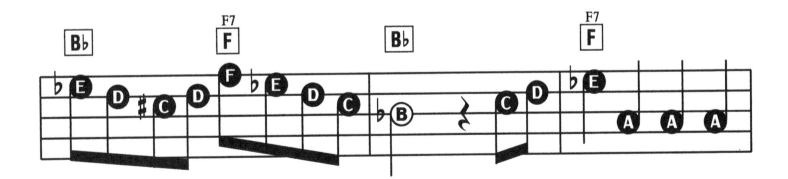

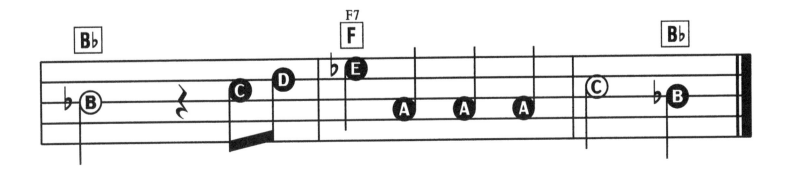

Piano Sonatina No. 1
In G Major
(First Movement Theme)

Registration 8

Ludwig Van Beethoven

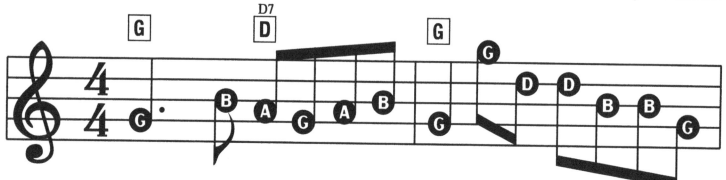

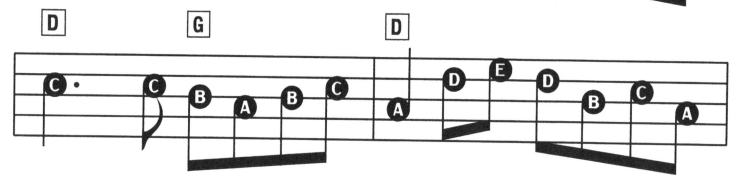

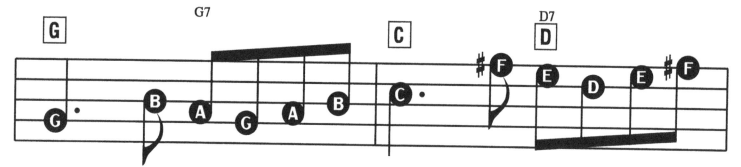

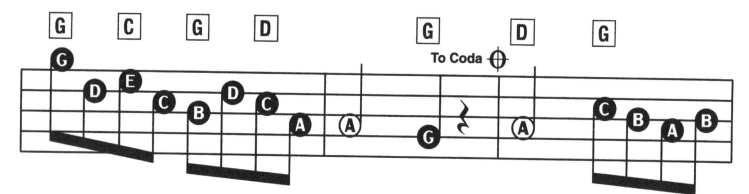

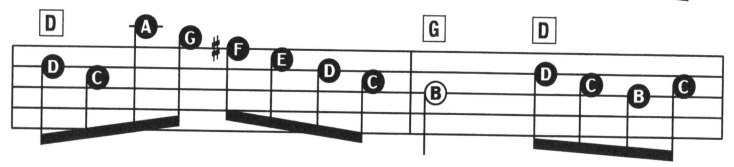

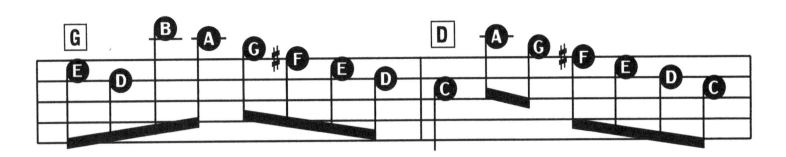

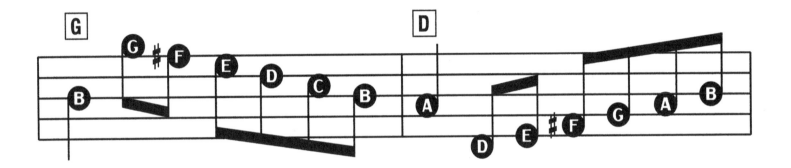

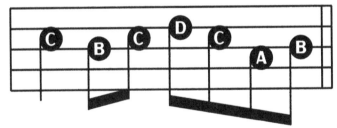

D.C. al Coda
(Return to beginning
Play to ⊕ and
Skip to Coda)

CODA

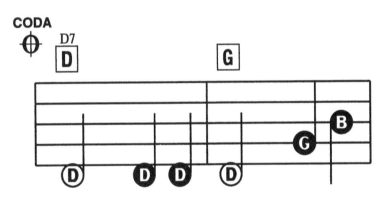

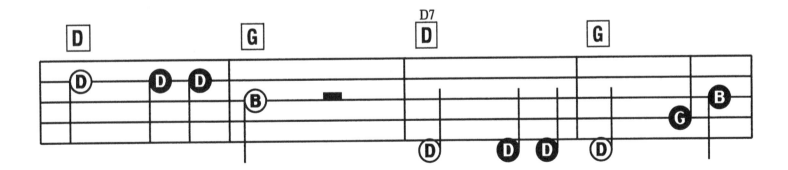

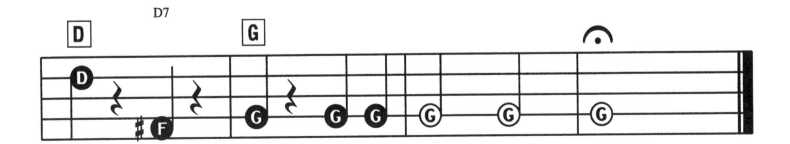

Septet
(Third Movement)

Registration 2
Rhythm: Waltz

Ludwig Van Beethoven

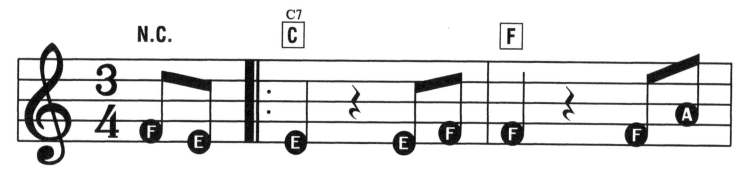

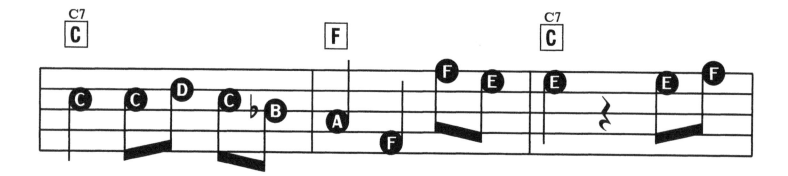

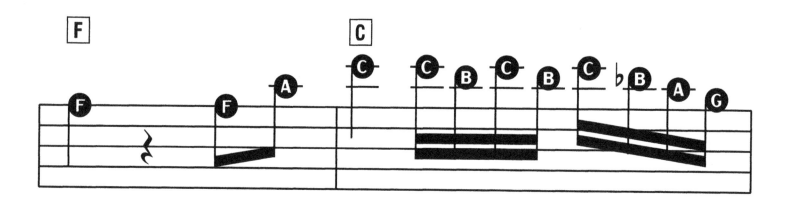

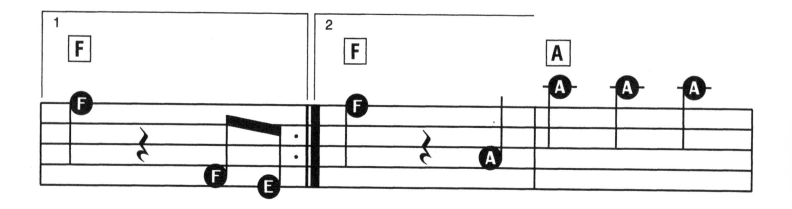

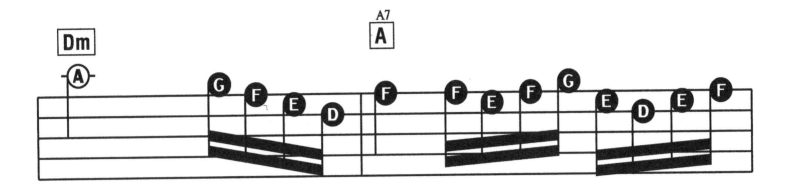

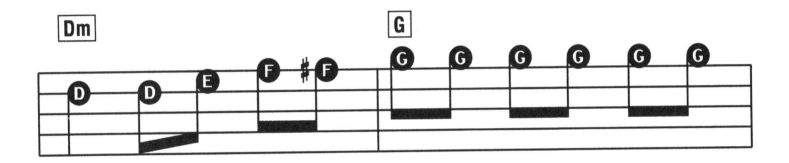

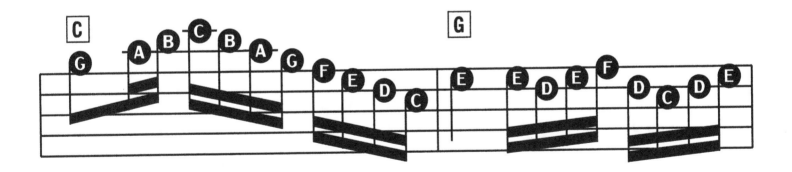

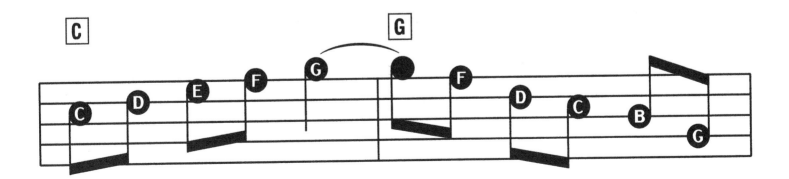

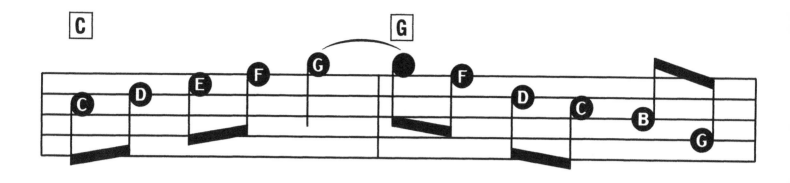

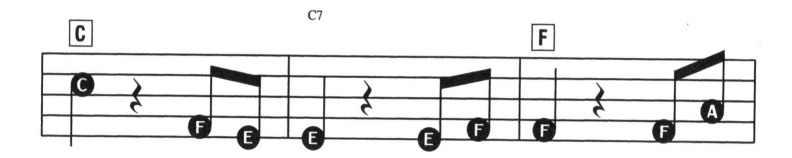

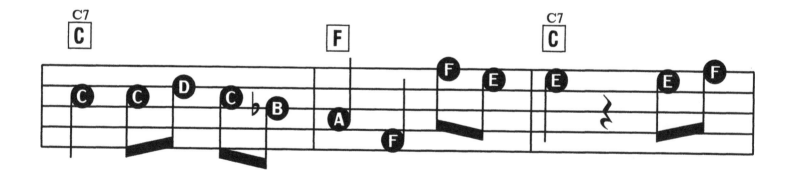

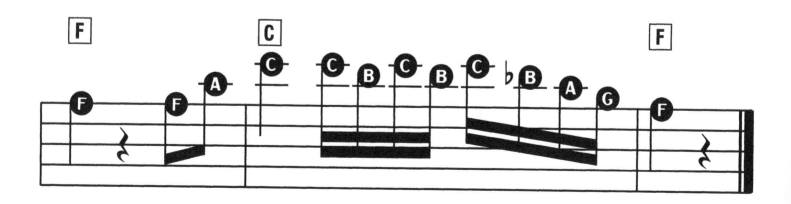

Symphony No. 5 In C Minor
(First Movement Theme)

Registration 3

Ludwig Van Beethoven

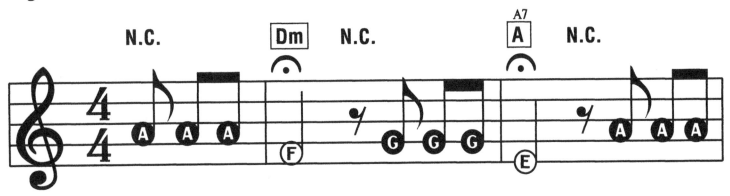

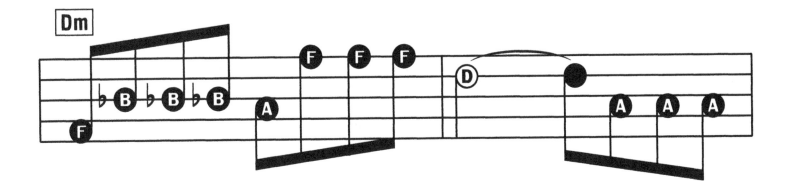

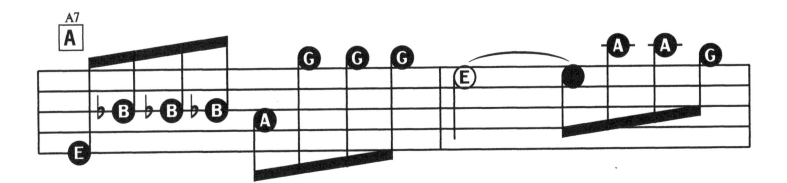

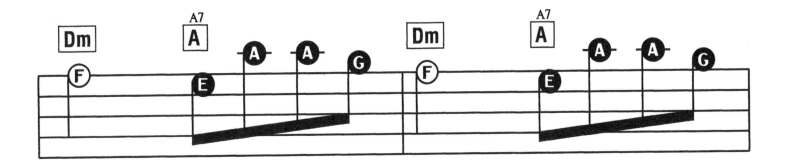

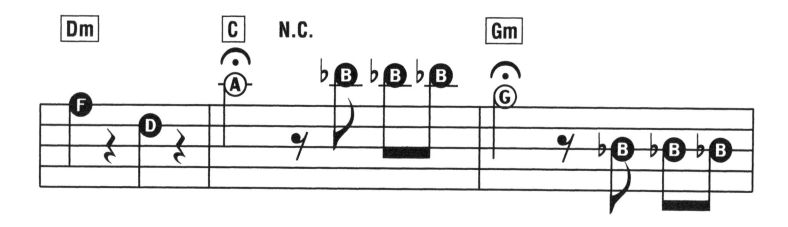

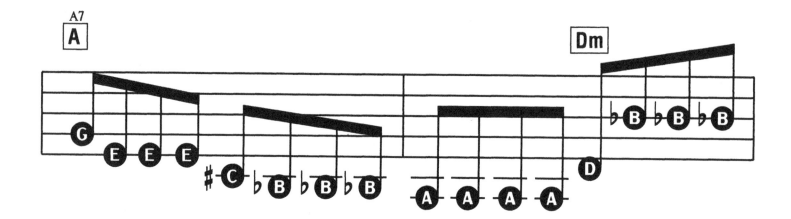

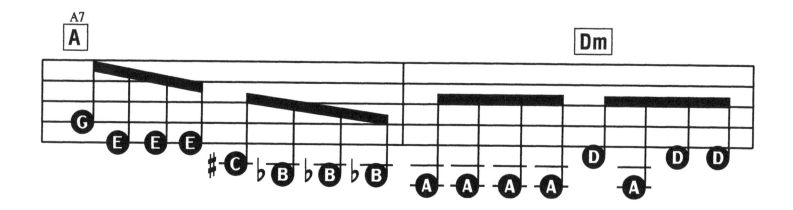

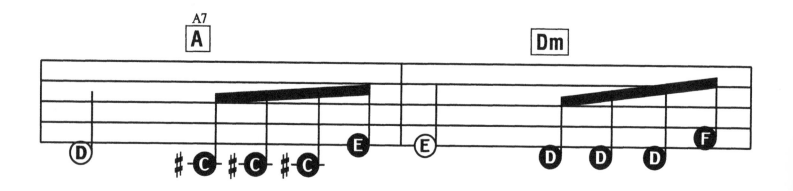

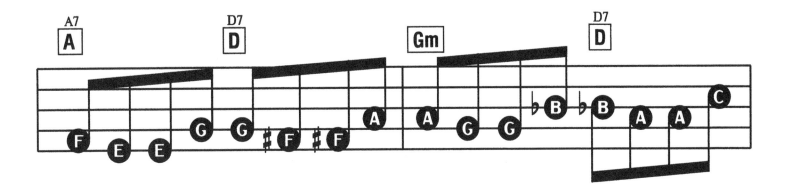

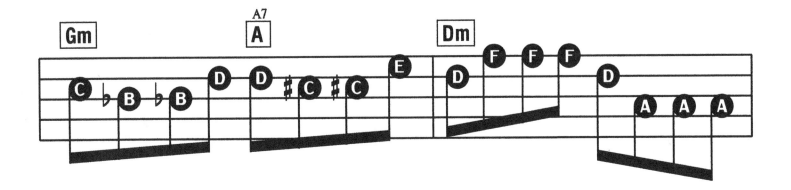

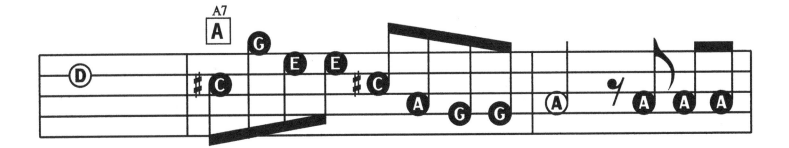

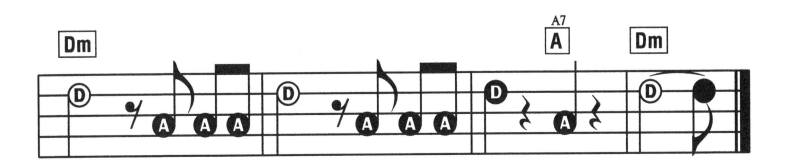

Symphony No. 9
(Fourth Movement, "Ode To Joy")

Registration 5
Rhythm: March

Ludwig van Beethoven

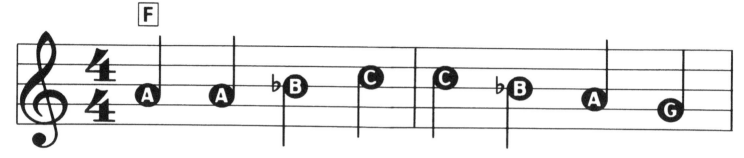

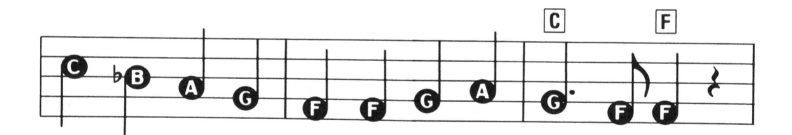

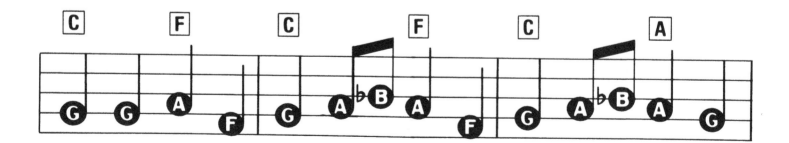

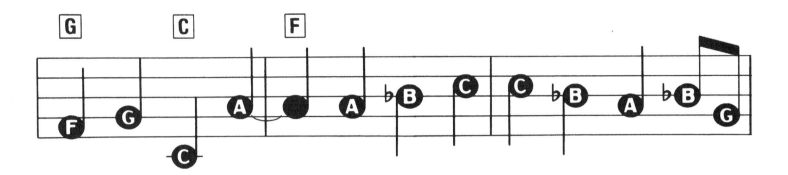

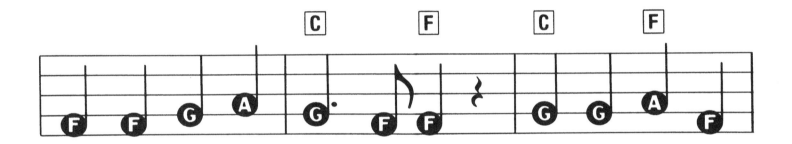

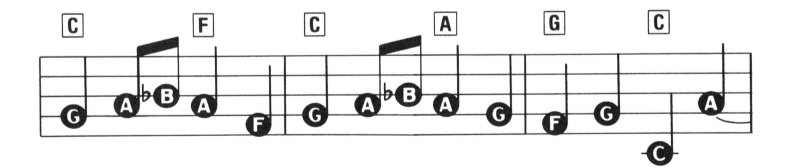

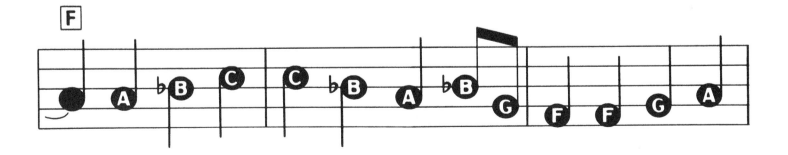

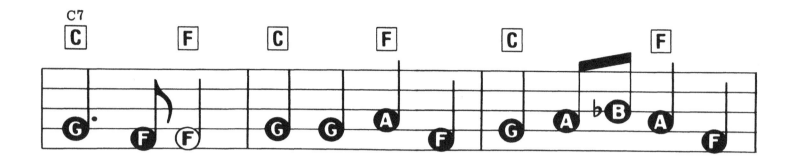

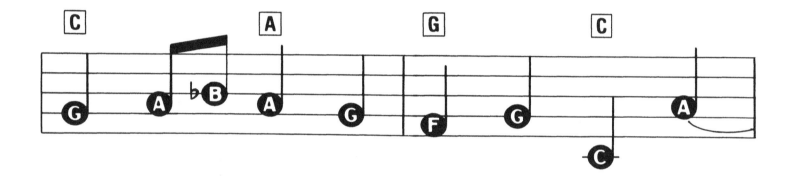

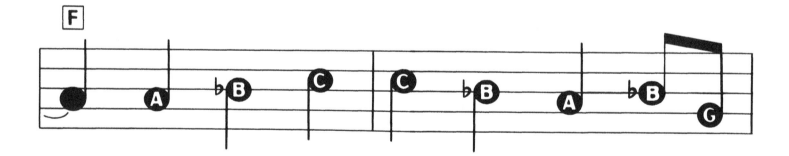

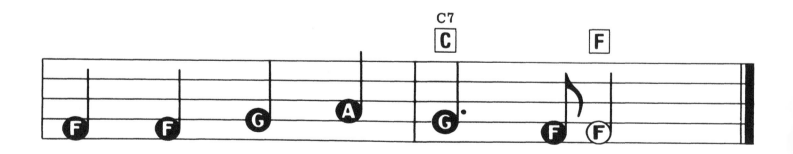

Intermezzo, Op. 118, No. 2

Registration 8

Johannes Brahms

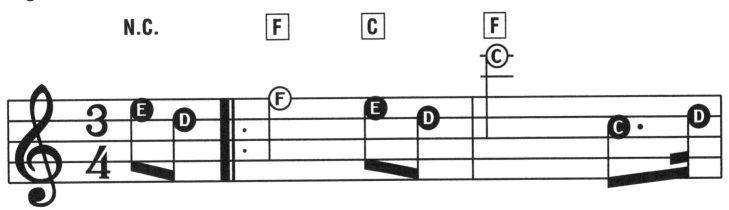

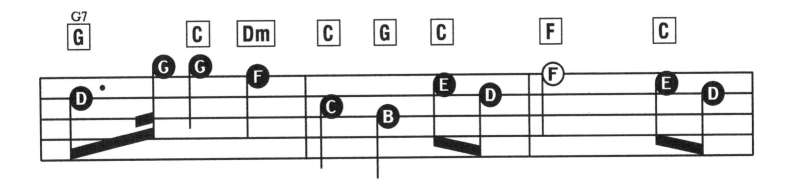

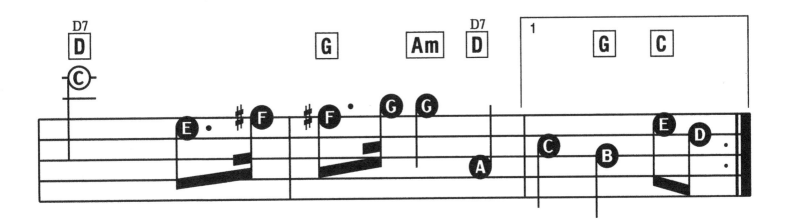

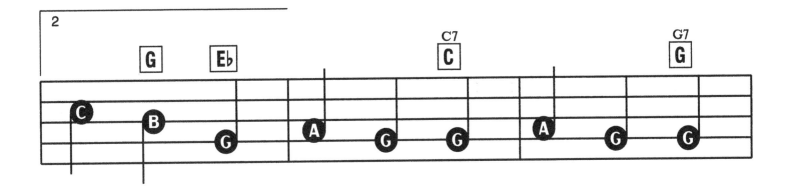

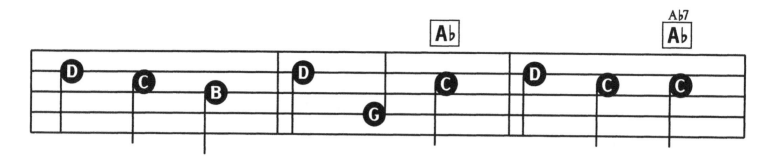

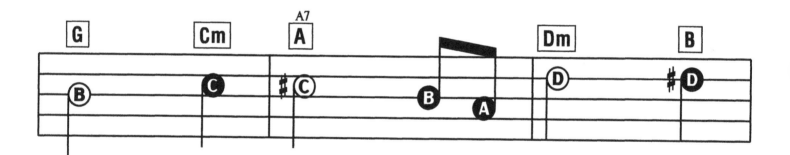

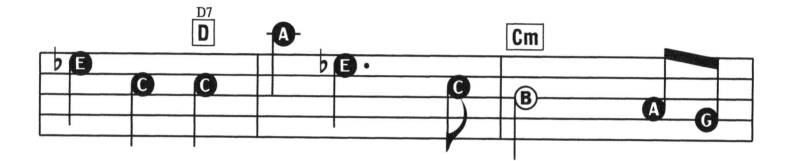

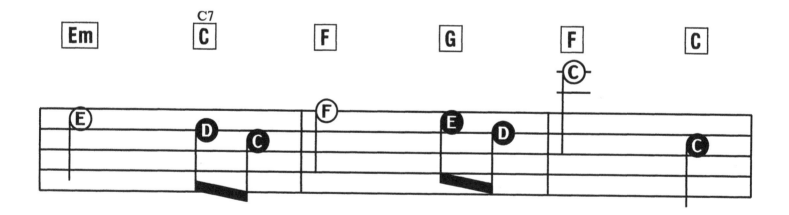

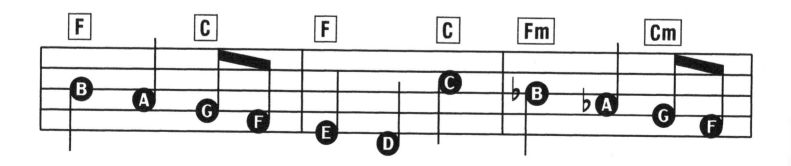

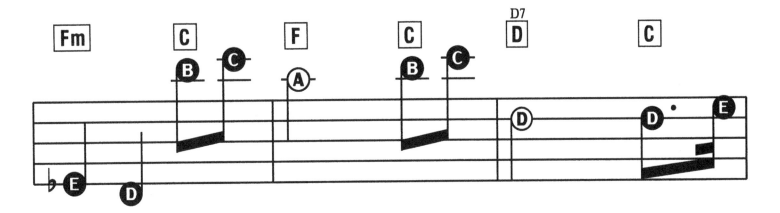

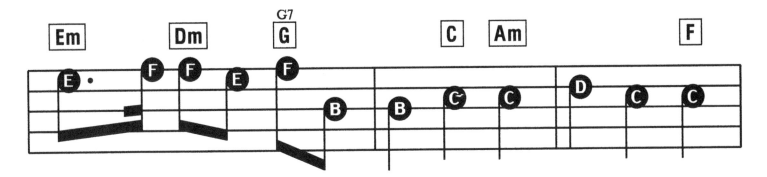

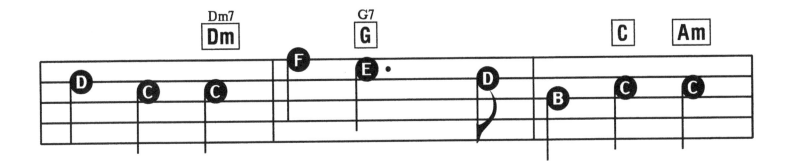

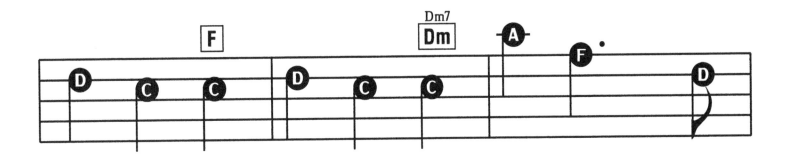

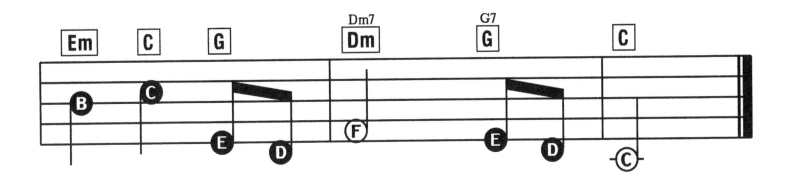

Academic Festival Overture

Registration 5

Johannes Brahms

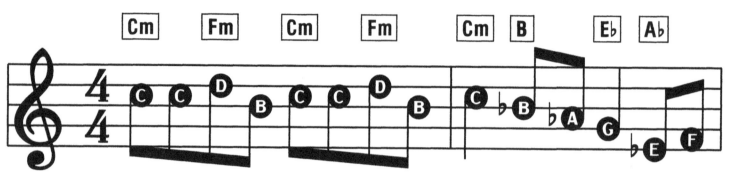

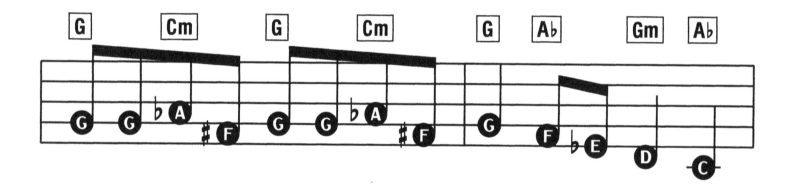

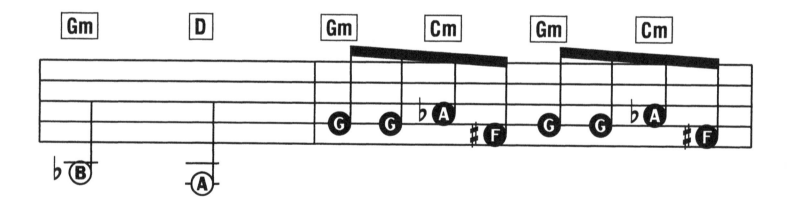

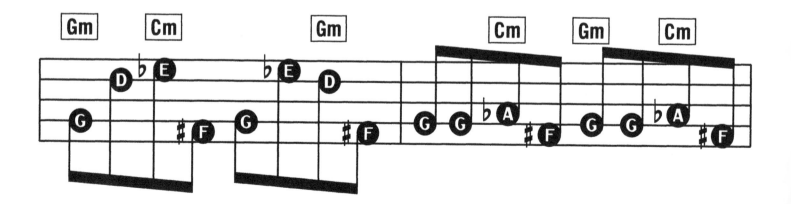

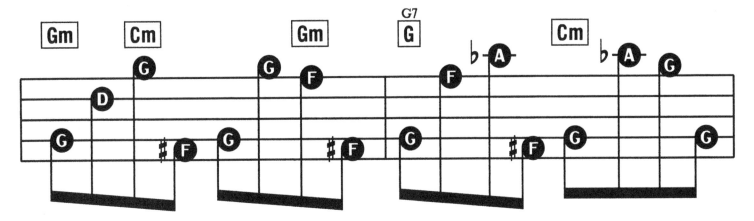

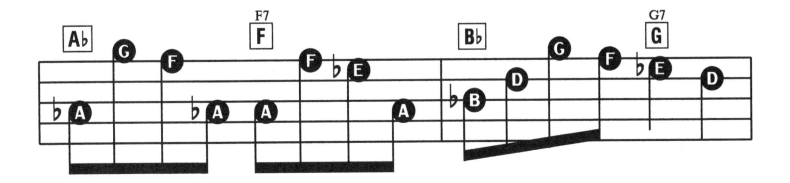

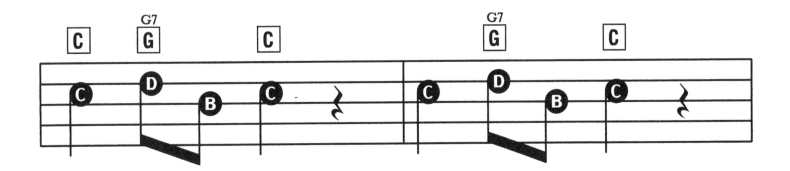

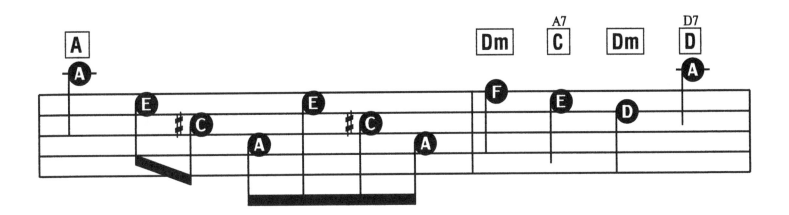

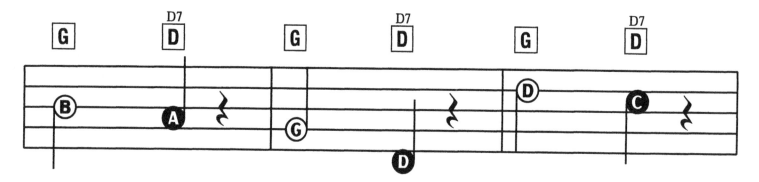

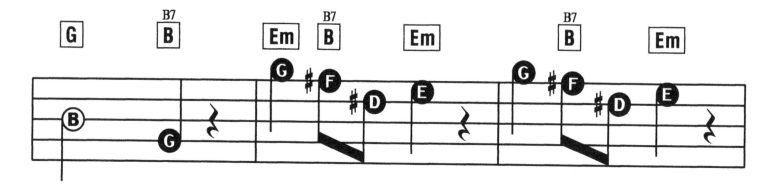

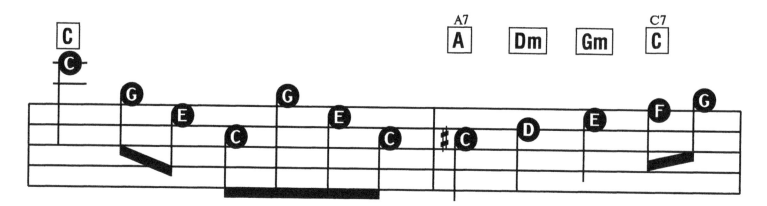

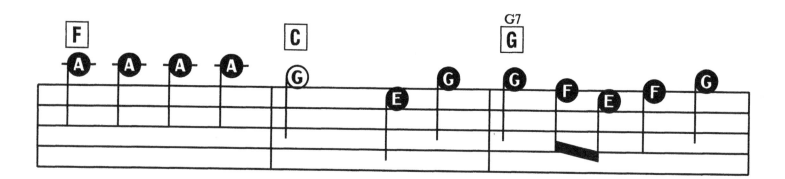

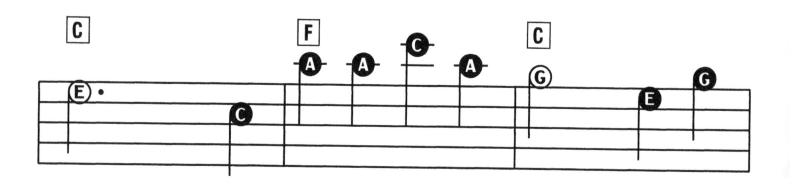

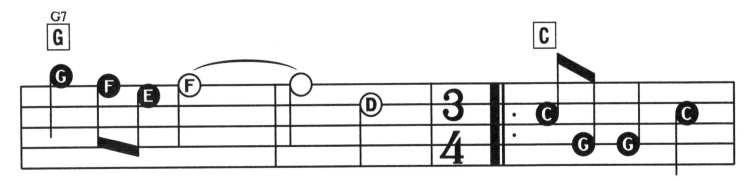

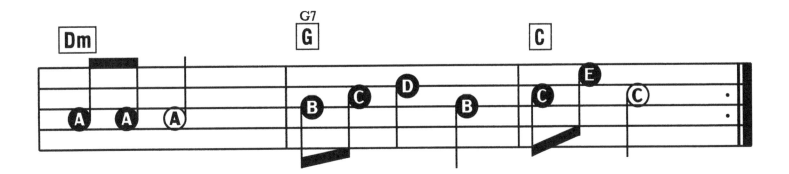

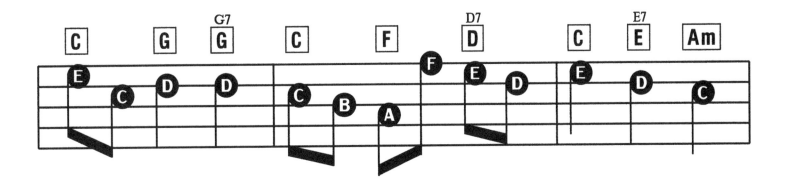

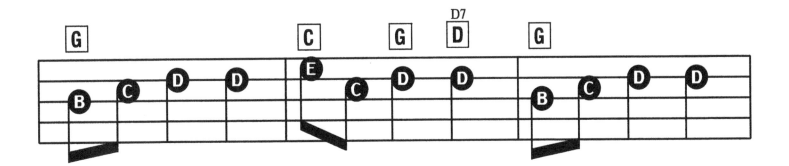

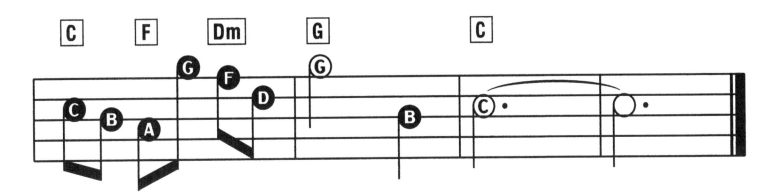

55

Ballade In G Minor, Op. 118, No. 3

Registration 8

Johannes Brahms

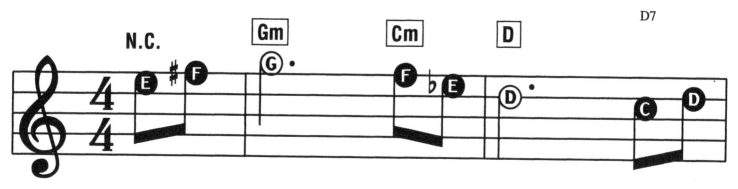

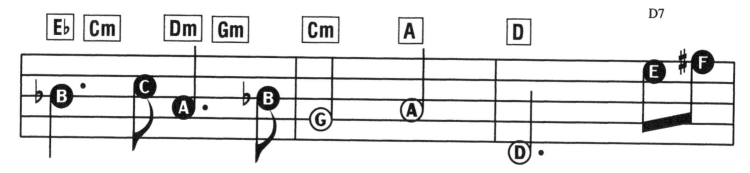

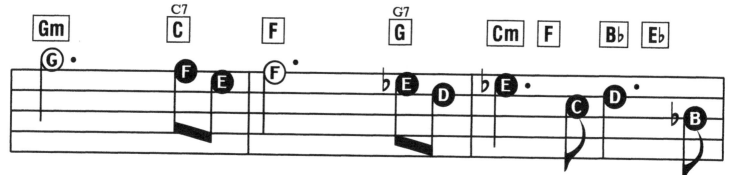

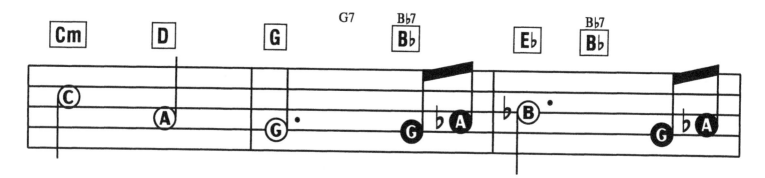

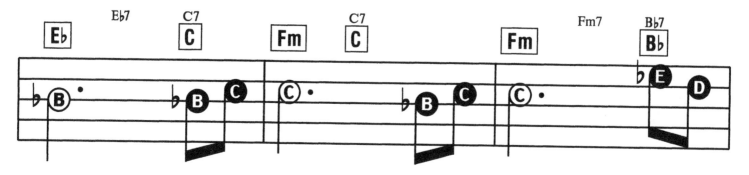

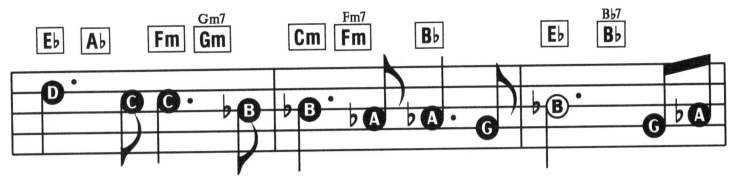

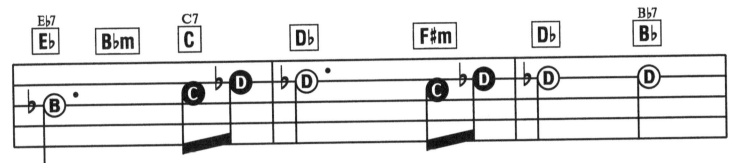

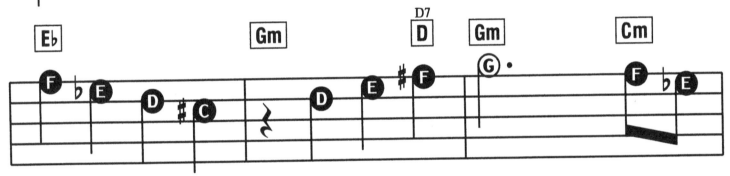

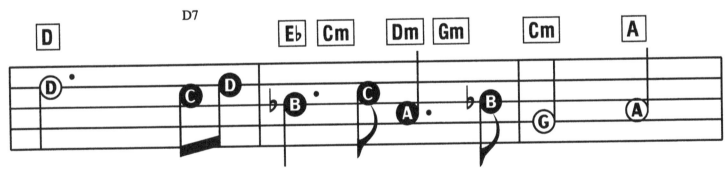

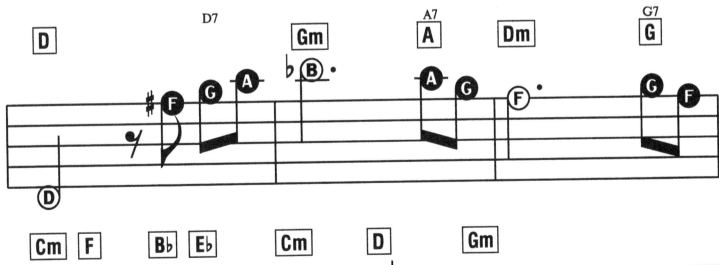

Hungarian Dance No. 5

Registration 10

Johannes Brahms

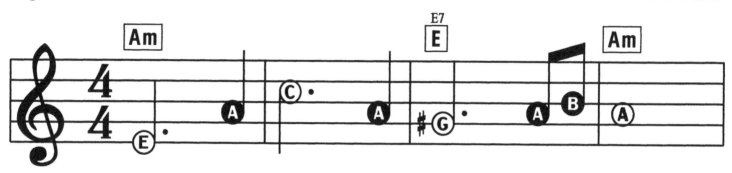

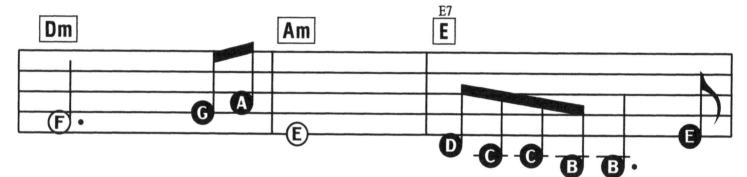

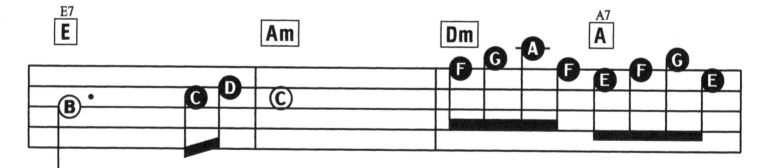

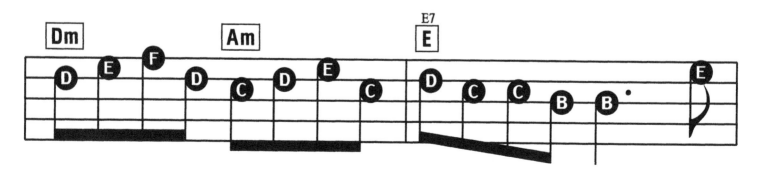

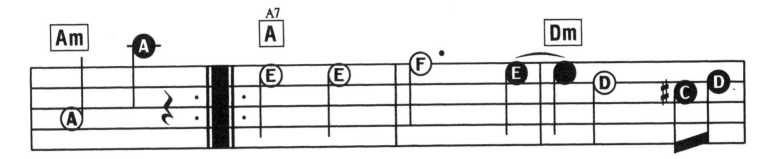

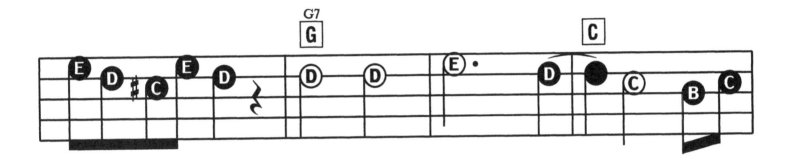

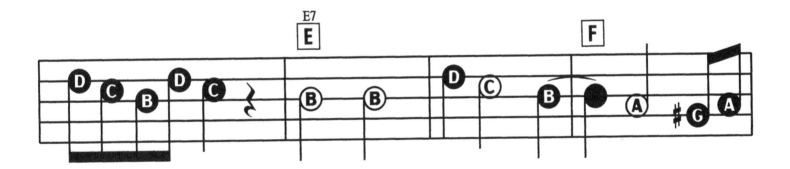

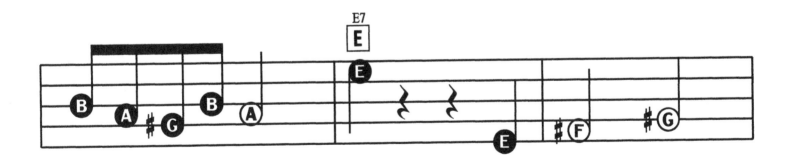

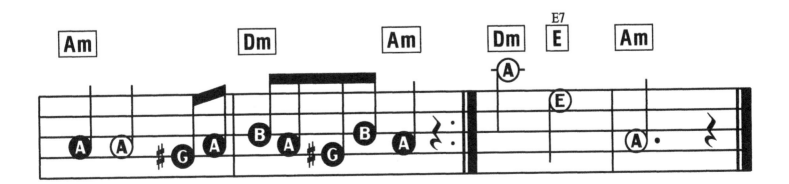

Intermezzo, Op. 117, No. 3

Registration 8

Johannes Brahms

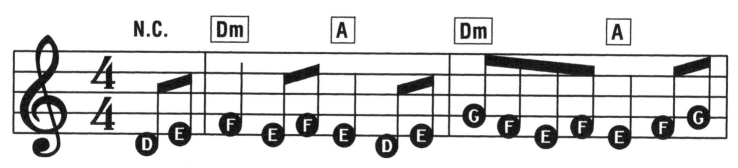

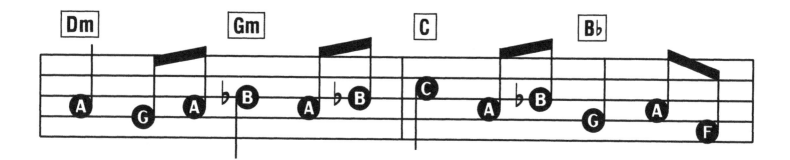

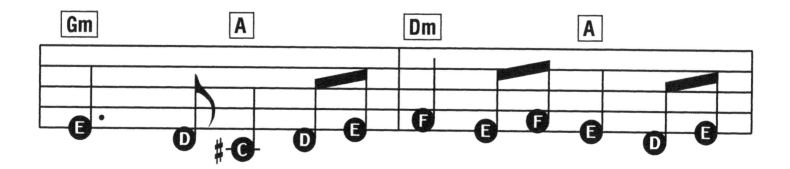

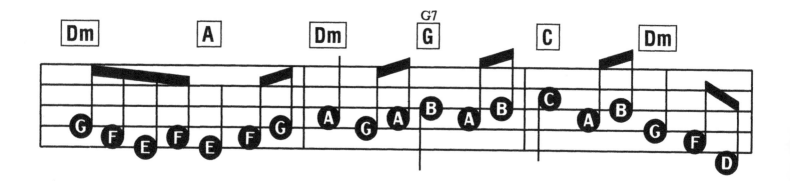

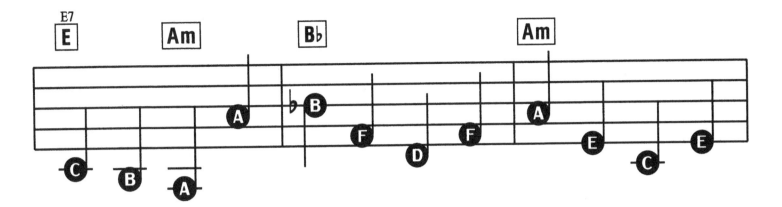

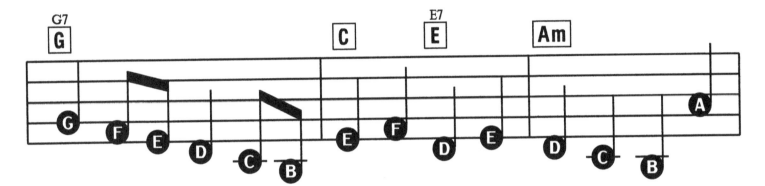

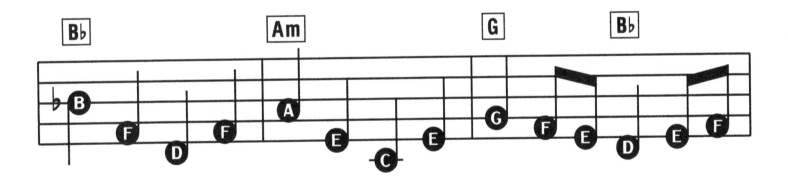

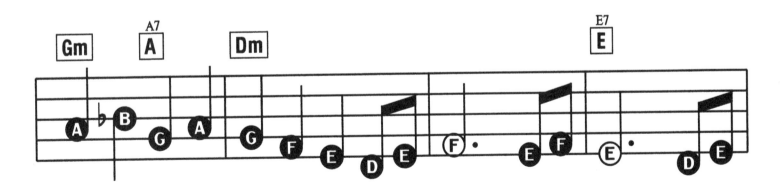

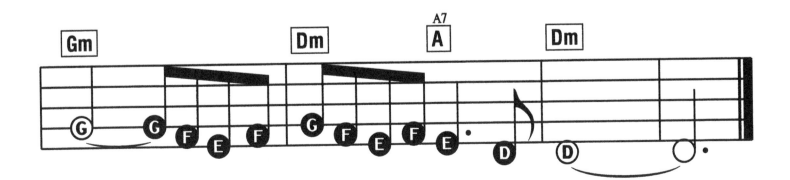

Lullaby
(Wiegenlied)

Registration 10
Rhythm: Waltz

Johannes Brahms

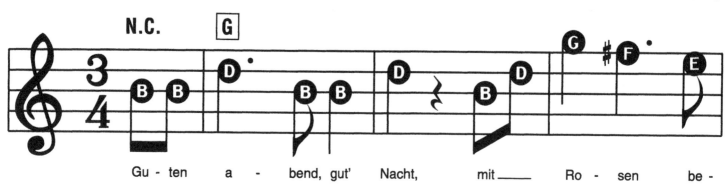

Gu - ten a - bend, gut' Nacht, mit ____ Ro - sen be -

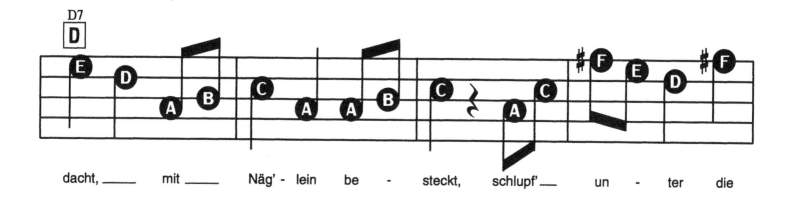

dacht, ____ mit ____ Näg' - lein be - steckt, schlupf' ____ un - ter die

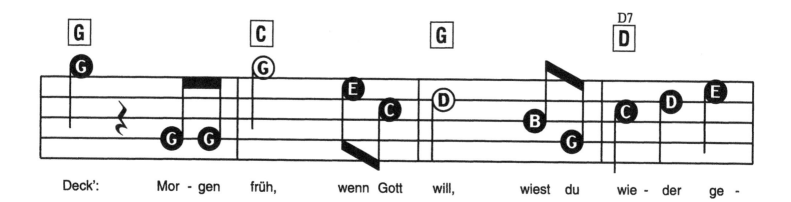

Deck': Mor - gen früh, wenn Gott will, wiest du wie - der ge -

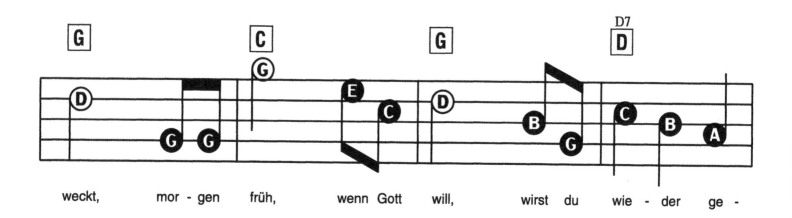

weckt, mor - gen früh, wenn Gott will, wirst du wie - der ge -

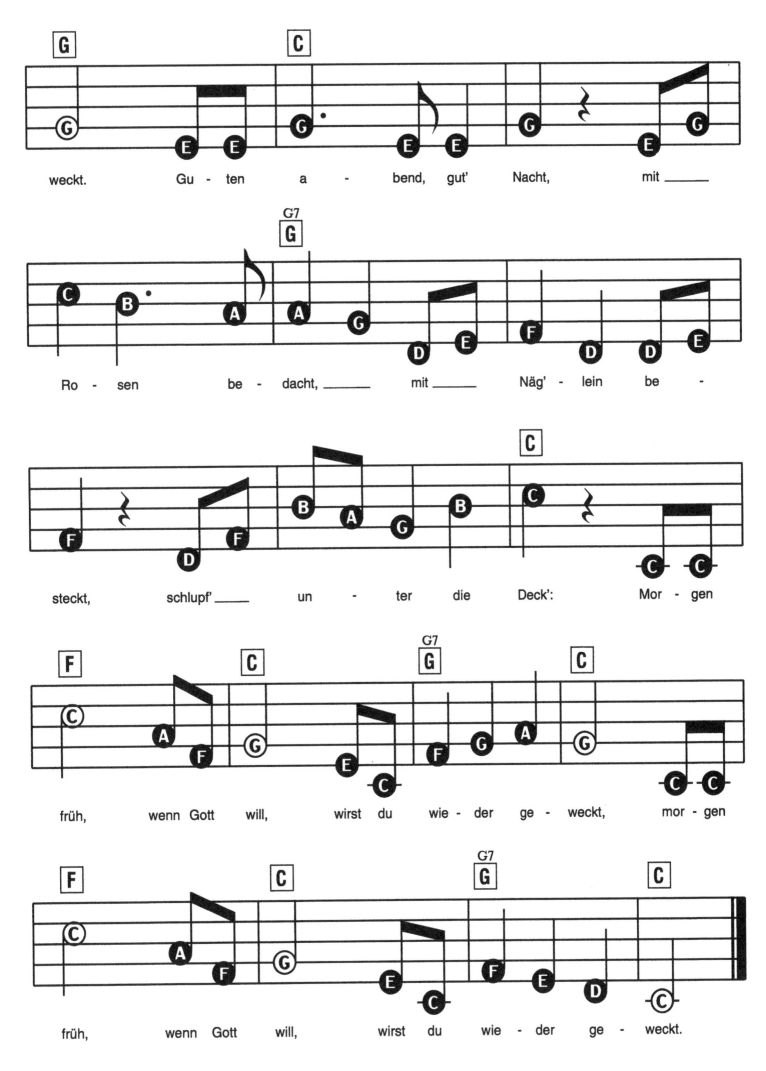

Symphony No. 1, Op. 68
(Fourth Movement Chorale)

Registration 3

Johannes Brahms

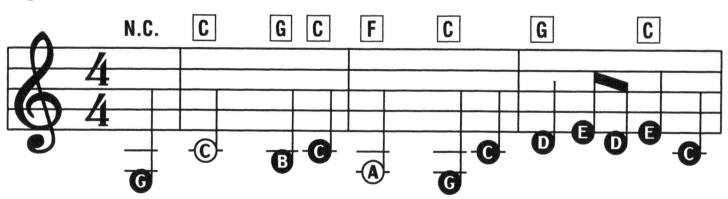

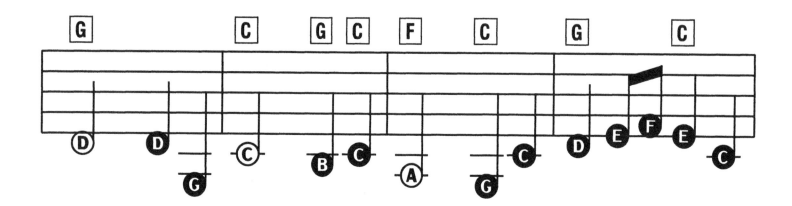

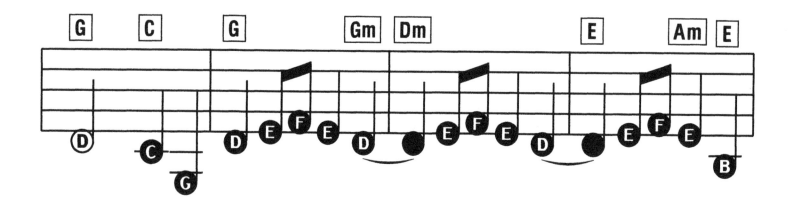

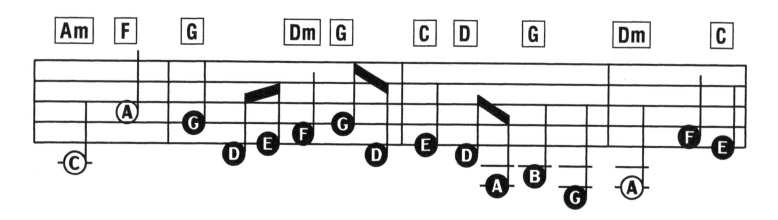

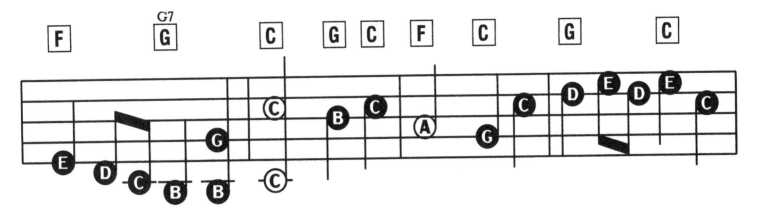

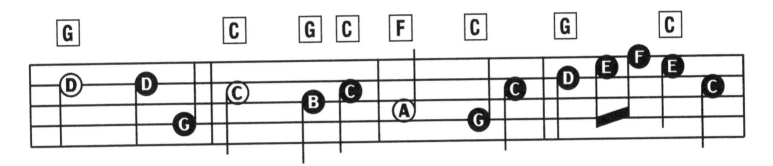

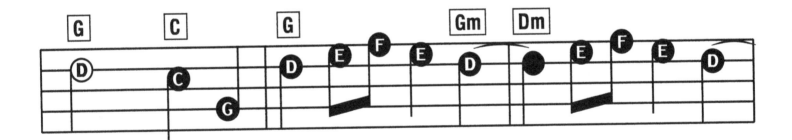

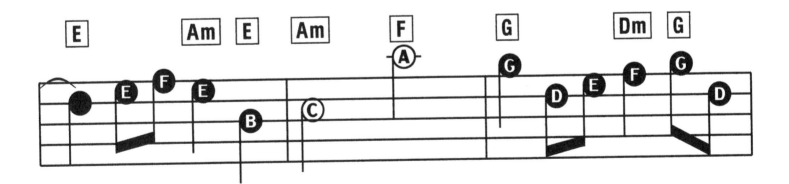

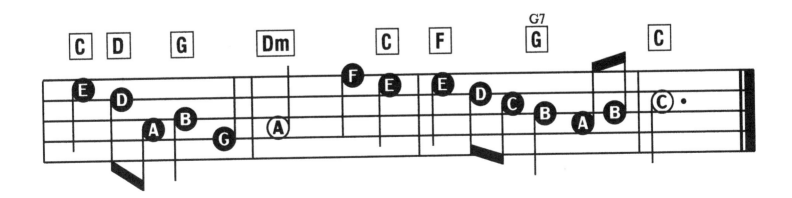

Waltz, Op. 39, No. 15

Registration 8
Rhythm: Waltz

Johannes Brahms

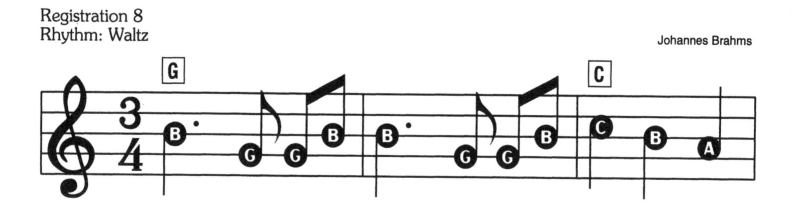

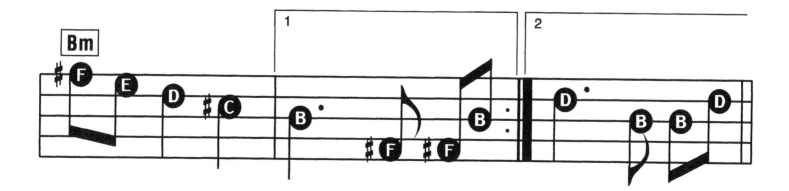

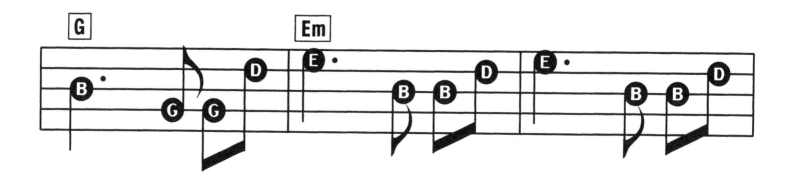

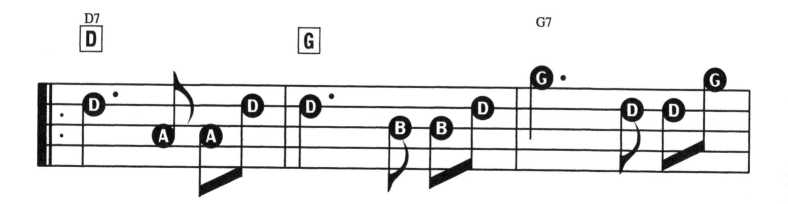

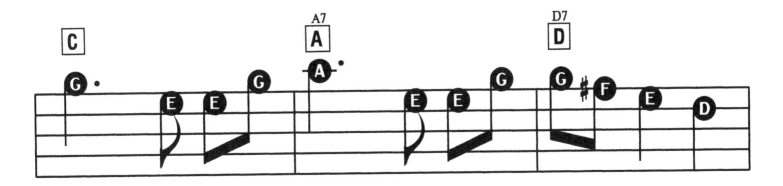
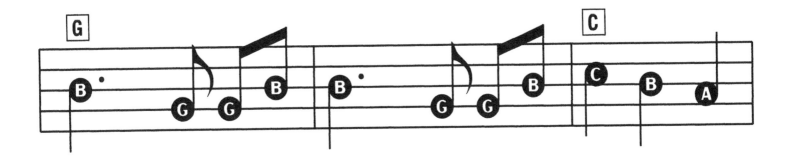
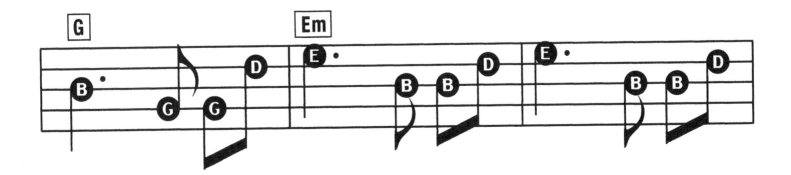
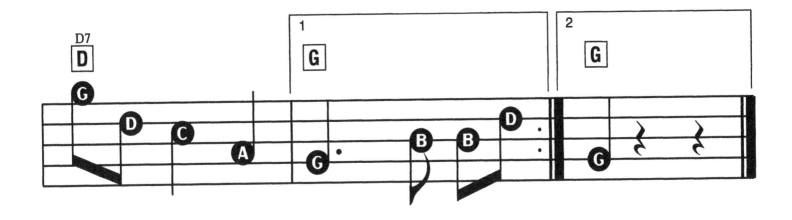

67

Wie Melodien

Registration 3

Johannes Brahms

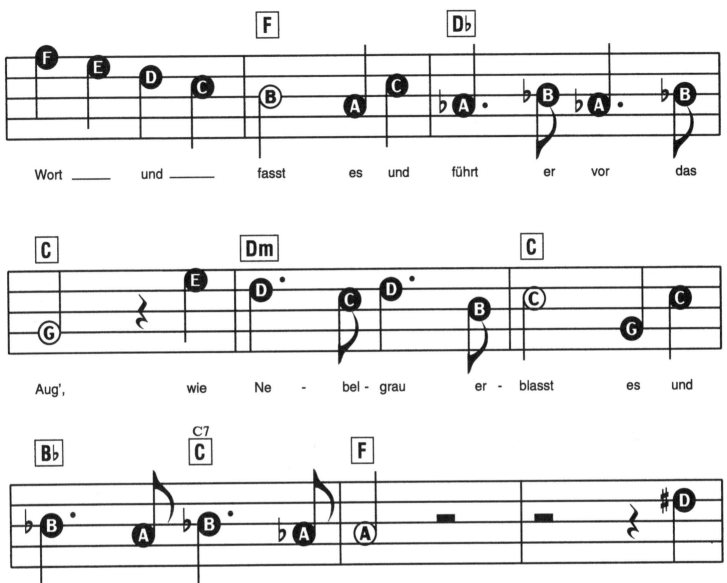

Wort _____ und _____ fasst es und führt er vor das

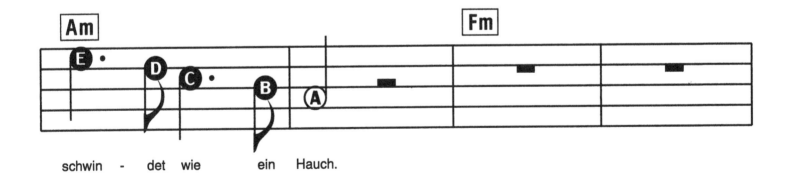

Aug', wie Ne - bel - grau er - blasst es und

schwin - det wie ein Hauch,   und

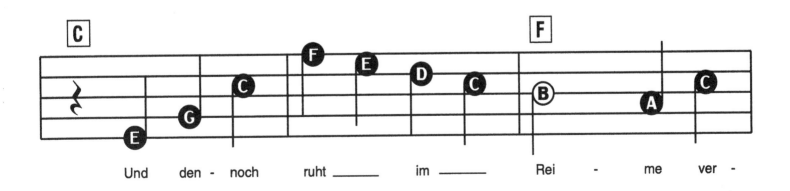

schwin - det wie ein Hauch.

Und den - noch ruht _____ im _____ Rei - me ver -

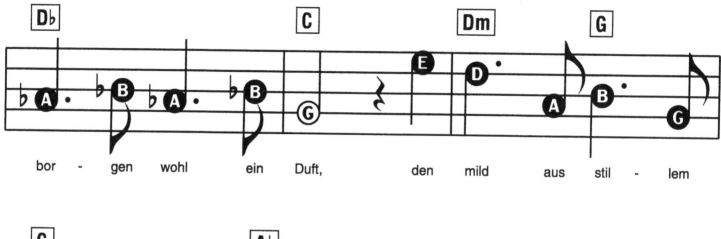

bor - gen wohl ein Duft, den mild aus stil - lem

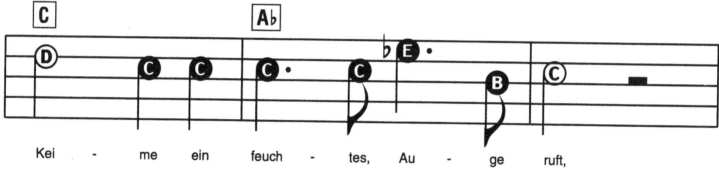

Kei - me ein feuch - tes, Au - ge ruft,

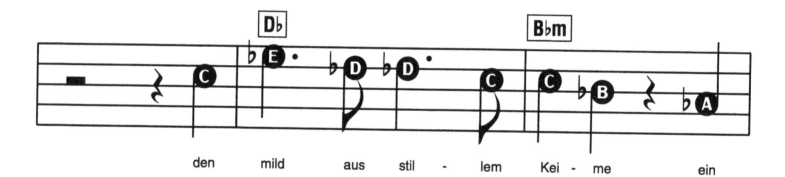

den mild aus stil - lem Kei - me ein

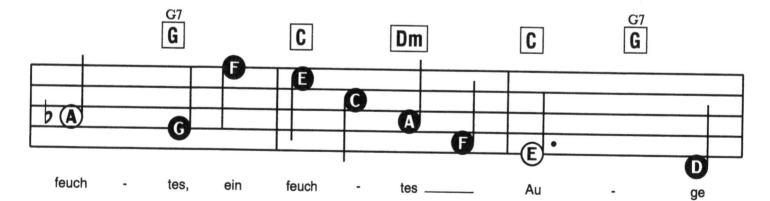

feuch - tes, ein feuch - tes _____ Au - ge

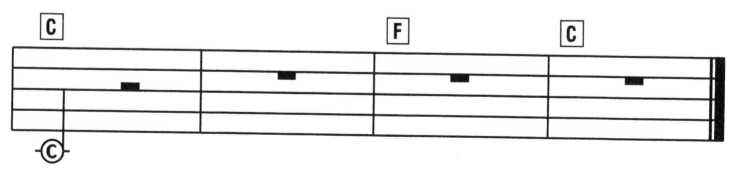

ruft.

Rhapsody, Op. 119, No. 4

Registration 8
Rhythm: March

Johannes Brahms

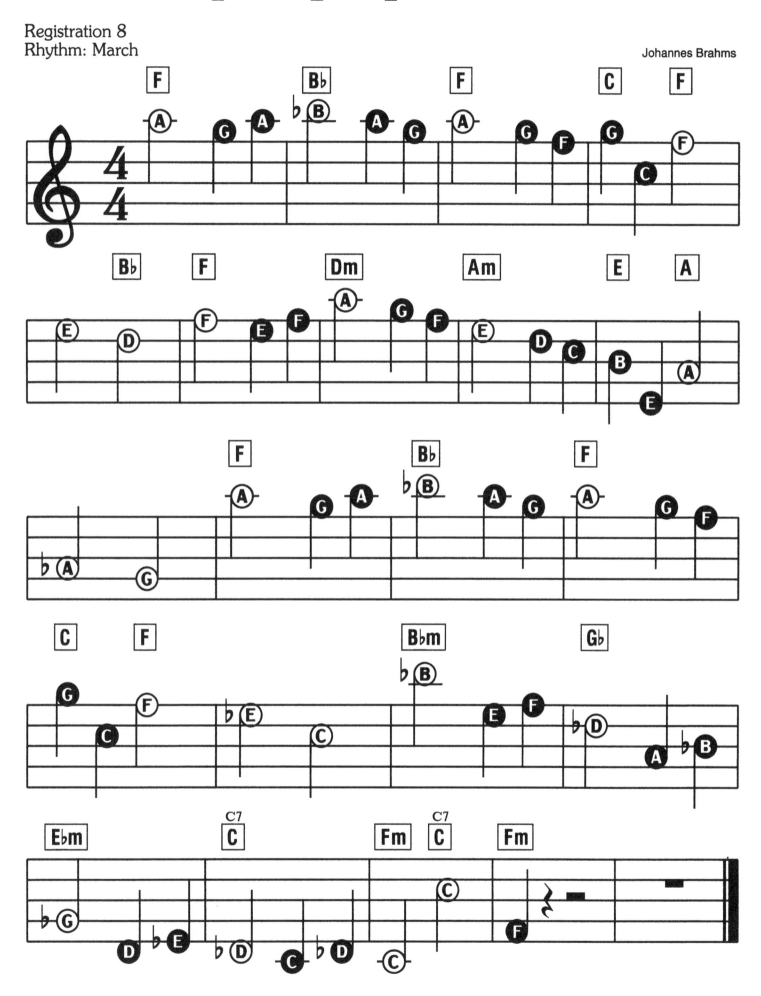

Registration Guide

- Match the Registration number on the song to the corresponding numbered category below. Select and activate an instrumental sound available on your instrument.

- Choose an automatic rhythm appropriate to the mood and style of the song. (Consult your Owner's Guide for proper operation of automatic rhythm features.)

- Adjust the tempo and volume controls to comfortable settings.

Registration

1	Flute, Pan Flute, Jazz Flute
2	Clarinet, Organ
3	Violin, Strings
4	Brass, Trumpet
5	Synth Ensemble, Accordion, Brass
6	Pipe Organ, Harpsichord
7	Jazz Organ, Vibraphone, Vibes, Electric Piano, Jazz Guitar
8	Piano, Electric Piano
9	Trumpet, Trombone, Clarinet, Saxophone, Oboe
10	Violin, Cello, Strings